SITTINGBOURNE
IN OLD PHOTOGRAPHS

SITTINGBOURNE CREEK as seen at the end of the last century. A barge under sail is coming in on the full tide, another is following in the distance and further barges are moored with sails furled. This scene was typical of everyday life on the north Kent shore and creeks eighty years ago and it is recaptured in spirit nowadays on occasions such as the annual barge race.

SITTINGBOURNE
IN OLD PHOTOGRAPHS

COLLECTED BY
ERIC R. SWAIN

ALAN SUTTON
1989

Alan Sutton Publishing Limited
Gloucester

First published 1989

Copyright © 1989 E.R. Swain

British Library Cataloguing in Publication Data

Sittingbourne in old photographs.
1. Kent. Sittingbourne, history
I. Swain, Eric R.
942.2'33
ISBN 0-86299-543-4

Typesetting and origination by
Alan Sutton Publishing.
Printed in Great Britain by
Dotesios Printers Limited.

CONTENTS

THIS POSTCARD VIEW OF MILSTEAD CHURCH was taken around 1910. Set in attractive countryside to the south of Sittingbourne, this church is dedicated to St Mary and the Holy Cross. The Victorian architect Butterfield was allowed to spoil the oldest part in his over-zealous restoration in 1872. Sir Stephen Glynne visited the church in 1850 and leaves a good pre-Butterfield description in his book *The Churches of Kent*, to which Archdeacon Harrison added the footnote in 1877, '. . . the whole church has been thoroughly restored . . .' (ouch!). Actually the nave and tower remain in unsullied Perpendicular style having escaped the attentions of Mr B.

INTRODUCTION

As with the companion work, *Faversham in Old Photographs*, this book also includes an area of countryside and villages around the central town; in this case Sittingbourne. There is inevitably a degree of interdependance between town and country, although perhaps in the case of Sittingbourne this relationship is less pronounced than with many English country towns. Historical circumstances provide the reason for this. Positioned astride the old Roman road from London to the Channel coast, Sittingbourne remained an insignificant settlement for centuries, overshadowed by its neighbour Milton Regis. Favoured by Saxon kings and important as a fishing port and potential barrier to invading Danes, Milton remained pre-eminent until it was challenged by, and eventually enveloped in, the gradual rise of Sittingbourne.

The increasing use of the old Roman route by pilgrims seeking miracles, solace or forgiveness at the shrine of Becket in Canterbury became a miracle for Sittingbourne in medieval times. The small village (as it was then) was centred between the bourne feeding the head of Milton Creek, and the Roman road which still forms the length of the High Street today, with West Street and East Street contiguous at either end. From the hill at Key Street the Roman surveyor's line may be seen in the present A2, forging with military directness through the middle of the town towards Canterbury, from whence it eventually arrived at Richborough near Sandwich. Sittingbourne thus became a convenient resting place for the medieval traveller and continued to offer hospitality to kings, queens and lesser folk alike until the present century. A number of well-known commodious inns and coaching houses became established in the High Street and some are featured in the following pages. By virtue of its situation on the main thoroughfare, Sittingbourne was able to outshine neighbouring Milton to the north and even Faversham to the east in the coaching business.

However, the coaching days waned as the railways revolutionized travel throughout the kingdom. Despite this, the development of Sittingbourne was maintained through industrial growth. For example, extensive deposits of fine brick earth have been excavated for the manufacture of bricks, leading to the lowering of much of the landscape by several feet. Fortunately it has been simple to replace the topsoil and reinstate the land for agricultural use, or even for building upon. Several fields in the area are below the level of the roads which separate them since the underlying brick earth was excavated long ago.

Occasionally this process can still be seen, for brickmaking is still continued in the area on a much reduced scale. Cement-making was also important for a time. One thousand tons per week were being produced in the 1900s and there are some huge disused quarries to the south of the town. Towards the end of the nineteenth century a paper-making mill was established on the north side of the railway, making use of the ready supply of water. The mills grew rapidly, converting Scandinavian forests into mountains of newspaper and becoming the major employer of labour in the town. The mills still cover a huge area and confirmed the trend for commerce and industry to be established on the north, i.e., the creek side, of the A2/High Street. On the south side, housing development has inevitably encroached on countryside which had extended remarkably close to the town centre as late as the 1920s and 1930s. Even today it is but a short drive from the High Street to reach the narrow lanes and villages on the gradually rising slope to the scarp of the North Downs.

The lower, generally more northern part of the sloping downs is good fertile land, suitable for fruit-growing for which it has become famous. This fruit belt stretches westwards to Rainham and eastwards to Faversham and the Canterbury area. Hops, which were once a prime crop also, are now grown in a very small proportionate amount compared with former years. The distribution of fruit and use of the hops was generally linked with the nearby towns. The southernmost part of the area covered by this book includes gradually rising ground, sometimes becoming clay cap overlying chalk, which is more suitable for arable farming, mixed with fruit in more favoured and fertile pockets. On this southern boundary of our area, villages and farmers traditionally looked towards Maidstone, Ashford and Faversham as being towns which were agriculturally more in sympathy with their rural way of life. Perhaps Sittingbourne was long regarded as the brash new boy of bricks and cement?

Roughly outlined, the geography of the area considered in this book extends from the Swale in the north, Iwade and Key Street to the west, Borden, Bredgar and Doddington to the south, and Lynsted with Teynham to the east. However, a strictly geographic representation of pictures has not been sought because, apart from the patchy availability of material making such an approach inadvisable, the purpose of the book is best served through a thematic presentation. The intention is to illustrate the life and times of the district during the past century or thereabouts.

For example, a selection of town and country churches is representative of the whole, samples of work and scenes in the villages show country life as it was throughout the rural area, and so on. Inevitably some areas are represented in the illustrations more often than others. This does not reflect on the relative importance of different communities, it is merely the chance result of the quantity and quality of photographs which have been available for use in this book. The aim throughout has been to create an impression within each section of the theme under review, not a street-by-street or village-by-village study.

There are undoubtedly collections of photographs in existence which did not become available for consideration in the compilation of this book. Surprisingly, not everything held on behalf of the public is easily accessible and, in the case of the county council libraries, where the staff are invariably most generous with their time and the assistance given towards helping the researcher, the cost of reproducing photographs in quantity is prohibitive. However, I do not think the present work has suffered through any of this, rather it is to be hoped that eventually a further publication would be possible, in which to include this additional material.

Free use has been made of postcard views, since the 'golden age' of the picture postcard during the first twenty years of this century left a wonderful record of life at that time.

Fortunately the decline in popularity of such cards has been compensated for, in part, by the availability of photographs taken privately. Source material of whatever form has been made available to me mainly through the generosity of private individuals, with the addition of further material held on behalf of the town by Mr Peter Morgan until facilities can be found for its proper storage and display. There are also some excellent pub photographs provided by Whitbreads. Proper acknowledgement is made at the end of this book.

Town and Buildings

THE JUNCTION OF HIGH STREET, Crown Quay Lane, East Street and Bell Road is at the point where a stream once flowed to the creek. In this picture a white-gloved traffic policeman stands before the shop of the London Bazaar which claimed to offer the 'finest selection in the World', and a wonderful small group of children with a pushchair stand at the corner anxiously awaiting the policeman's direction to cross the road. The junction is still an uncertain place to cross on foot and is rather less attractive now than in this view with its variety of horse-drawn vehicles. The London Bazaar has been replaced by a cinema.

HIGH STREET EAST, SITTINGBOURNE.

IN THE FIRST QUARTER OF THIS CENTURY photographers were still enough of a novelty to cause passers-by to stop and stare – or was it perhaps that they were aware that one should stand still in front of the camera? In this instance at the bottom of the High Street, with St Michael's Church on the right and Hulburd's on the left, the younger people stood still and most of the older people continued walking. Small deliveries were by carrier cycle, larger ones by horse-drawn cart, no motor vehicles were visible at a time when they were still a rarity, and babies surveyed the passing scene from on high in their large-wheeled perambulators.

Sittingbourne. High Street.

AN EARLIER AND WIDER VIEW OF THE HIGH STREET shown on the facing page. Taken in around 1905, this photograph shows Baldock's grocery shop on the left with Alfred Reynolds auctioneers and house furnishing premises beyond. There follows the low façade of Hulburds store (then 'wholesale and retail provision merchants ... drapers, milliners and undertakers ... insurance agents', etc.) opposite the tree-filled graveyard of St Michael's. Returning down the street, a most handsome horse and carriage is outside Boulding's butchers shop and nearer, under the sun blinds, can be seen the windows of Daly's the milliners who not only offered 'mantles, millinery and furs at moderate prices' but would also trim bonnets and hats free of charge!

LOOKING EAST DOWN THE HIGH STREET in the early 1900s with the Rose Inn (see page 110) and the Bull Hotel (page 119) on the right vying with each other in their window-box displays. The Georgian façade on the left is the old Ballards Hotel building (see page 110) and the two-bayed house on the right is Brenchley House, formerly a school. A pony and trap enjoyed untroubled parking on the left, and the lady with the bicycle regarded the photographer from the middle of the road without needing to be concerned about the traffic.

THIS PRE-FIRST WORLD WAR VIEW westwards up the High Street shows that the Bull Hotel had a garage with a pit which would have been a fairly modern (and necessary) facility at the time. Outside there was a handsome gas lamp, doubtless one of the 196 which, in 1909, the Sittingbourne Gas Company lit at a cost of £3 2s.6d. per lamp per annum. Further on can be seen the clock of the old Town Hall, while on the opposite side of the street can be seen the signs of the Lion Hotel and the Rose Inn. On the far right the slow shutter speed of the camera is demonstrated by the blurred image of the running children.

High St. Sittingbourne. W3395.

THE HIGH STREET at about its mid point, as seen in the early part of the century. On the far left the building with columned porch is now occupied by Barclays Bank and beyond that stood the old Town Hall. This building with its impressive porch and clock tower, was built as the corn exchange in 1859 and converted to use as a town hall some 20 years later. The illustration shows two fine gas-lamp standards on the pavement outside the main entrance. Further on the two-storey buildings were demolished to make way for the building of Central Avenue and a new Town Hall was later erected in this road. Subsequently the old Town Hall building was also demolished to be replaced by a characterless façade fronting another bank, shops and offices. The church spire is that of the Congregational Church built in 1844 with a distinctive spire which remains a High Street landmark (see page 18 top).

THE HIGH STREET looking east with the entrance to Berry Street on the near left separating two clothing shops, the nearest of which formed part of Cobden Place (see page 16). This view is similar in period or earlier to that on the facing page – probably around 1900 – and the deep kerb with a step for pedestrians can be clearly seen on the south side of the road. This picture was evidently taken a little after noon on a day when the shops were open, yet most of the street was singularly empty with the appearance of the photographer being an event unusual enough to engage the attention of the few passers-by. Occasionally a building can be recognised when comparing this picture with the present High Street but much of the south side seen here has been lost to fairly recent change leading, it has to be said, to a less attractive frontage.

A POSTCARD SENT IN 1907 reveals a distinctly more busy scene in that part of the High Street also shown on page 15. The first turning on the left is Berry Street and the first three shops this side comprised Cobden Place. From right to left they were: May & Sayers at No.100, hosiers and outfitters ('. . . men's suits from 35/- . . . school outfits a specialite.' [sic]); The London Central Meat Co. (seen here with an aproned butcher at the door); The Rendezvous Inn. Nearer still can be seen the sign of Bennetts, oil and colour merchants. On the opposite (south) side, by a shop with three bracketed gas lamps to illuminate the window display from outside, a group of fashionably dressed ladies pass by, perhaps having just left Minters Tea Rooms, the angled sign of which may be discerned further down the road.

A LATER VIEW OF THE HIGH STREET than those previously shown (cf. page 12), this was the subject of a postcard used in 1920. The signs of the Lion Inn and Rose Inn can be seen on the left, and nearer still is a glimpse of the building which first housed Vallance and Payne's Bank and later became Martin's, which in turn became Barclay's. A building society now occupies the premises. Here the cyclist looks surprisingly modern, yet the schoolgirls and ladies opposite were wearing long skirts and straw hats. As they passed the open display of Webb's fish shop, a road sweeper pursued an apparently losing battle in trying to cope with the distinctly mucky surface. Perhaps it was frustration that caused him to leave his handcart near the centre of the road, forcing the approaching horse and cart to steer well over to the wrong side as it passed the Bull Hotel.

THE CENTRE OF THIS PICTURE reveals the unattractive body of the Congregational Church (see page 14) faced by the imposing stone front and spire. To the left are the buildings formerly occupying the site of the present Central Avenue. To the right of the church stands the home and office of Hedley Peters 'auctioneer, valuer, estate and emigration agent' (and incidentally, captain extraordinary of the fire brigade, of which more later). This building is No. 93 and is still in use as an estate agency.

TAKEN FROM THE TOP OF THE CHURCH TOWER in around 1900, this photograph shows, in the immediate foreground, the roofs of the shop with a house behind that formerly bordered the path to the Butts at the western end of the churchyard (see page 20 top). Other prominent buildings referred to on previous pages can be identified, but by far the most striking feature of this illustration is the glimpse it affords of the open fields to the west and south of the High Street. The rural character of Sittingbourne, which developed out of its favourable position on the main coastal route with close proximity to the tidal and navigable head of the creek, was demonstrably evident as late as the early years of this century, although of course the view to the north, out of sight to the right of this picture, would have encompassed paper mills and the vast brickfields beyond the railway station.

Bottom, left.
LOOKING WEST UP THE HIGH STREET in 1908. On the left of this photograph may be seen the angled shop window of The International Grocers and across the road is the dominating building of the London and County Bank (now occupied by the Halifax Building Society). Returning down the north side, there was Taylor & Son, jewellers and silversmiths, next was Shepherd Neame's Three Post Boys Inn followed by the arched opening to Smeed's Yard. Interested onlookers stood in the doorway of Bishop & Sons, painters, plumbers and gasfitters. Their windows appeared full of attractive brass gas and oil lamps, and the firm also carried on business as builders and contractors with premises which still remain in Albany Road.

THE CHURCHYARD OF ST MICHAEL'S still has a path at the western end (see page 19) which led from The Butts and St Michael's Road to the High Street where, as can be seen here, the opening was lit by another of those 196 splendid gas lamps possessed by Sittingbourne in 1907. On the west side of the path was the shop of John Hampden Whibley, draper and outfitter ('. . . agent for the celebrated BOUN-TU-FIT suits.') with a private house behind.

A LAST LOOK DOWN THE HIGH STREET again in the 1900s, from the commencement of West Street. On the right (south) side there is the Baptist Church (see pages 152 bottom and 153) and beyond there was a number of large trees which evidently grew in the front gardens of the properties collectively numbered 121, but named 'The Lawn', 'Cedars' and 'Polveners'. Some of these properties survived until 1988 before being finally demolished after having previously served as premises for Sittingbourne Fire Brigade. In the distance the distinctive landmarks of the Congregational Church spire and Town Hall clock tower may be seen. On the left of the picture is the opening to Station Street with the corner shop of John French, chemist and optician.

THE STOCK MARKET was described in Edwardian times as one of the best known in the county. The market was held by Mr F. Austen Bensted on alternate Mondays and was situated on the paddock at the rear of the Bull Hotel. (Now the DHSS car park). The stock market has been discontinued but the area on the north side of the football ground is still used for an open general market.

THE SWIMMING BATHS AND GYMNASIUM pictured here was built in 1896 by public subscription although it was recorded that the bulk of the cost of over £2,000 was obtained from Mr Frank Lloyd and family (see page 39). Swimming was discontinued in the winter months when a floor was laid to provide a surface for gymnastics and roller skating. The building was situated at The Butts next to the old Latimer Congregational Chapel which had been converted for use by Sittingbourne Working Men's Club and Institute.

HIGH STREET WEST, SITTINGBOURNE.

THIS ASPECT OF WEST STREET, in around 1910, had many features which may be identified in the present buildings. The ivy-clad wall on the left is part of the police station (now the magistrate's court) on the corner of Park Road, opposite was The Railway Tavern (now re-named the Ypres Tavern) on the corner of Pembury Street. The Edwardian dress of the figures and the quiet air of the street contrast sharply with this traffic-burdened part of the town today.

Bottom, right.
WEST STREET from the start of London Road, looking east. This view is from a card posted in 1905 and shows a horse and waggon carrying wicker baskets leaving Hawthorn Road on the left. Other horse-drawn vehicles may be seen, including one of Cremer's delivery vans bearing their name and a picture of a soda syphon. W.J. Cremer & Sons Ltd. were bakers, confectioners and mineral water manufacturers. A garage now occupies the site of the large former building opposite the prominent Roman Catholic Church of the Sacred Heart which was built two years earlier in 1903.

THIS VIEW OF WEST STREET is a little further west than the previous illustration, the turning on the left is William Street. The date appears to have been around 1930 with some early motor vehicles (possibly a Bull-nosed Morris in the foreground) and a motor cycle combination. About a decade later heavy damage was caused by Second World War bombing, when some of the shops and buildings on the north side of the street were destroyed.

WEST STREET, SITTINGBOURNE

THE END OF WEST STREET looking west towards Holleybank Hill in around 1950. The shops, church and houses are the same buildings pictured 50 years earlier on the previous page. Motor vehicles were more numerous of course and of an appearance well-remembered by many today. Street furniture is also of a different form from that of earlier years; clear bus stop signs on concrete posts and electric street lamps (note the one suspended centrally on a wire above the road).

THE VIEW FROM WEST STREET, looking south up Park Road, shows the police station on the left and the creeper-covered premises of Pullen's Garage opposite. Mr W.J. Pullen was a versatile mechanic (see page 89) and maintained many of the earliest cars in the district. The premises were bombed in the Second World War during the same air-attack referred to on the previous page. This illustration is from a view taken in around 1920, when the corner shop was the 'Times Printing Office'.

PARK ROAD in around 1910 was favoured by many tradesmen and middle-class citizens who lived in the large 'villas' built there not many years previously. The tall tower on the right belongs to Garfield House, supposedly built for a local barge-owner who was able to climb to the tiny room in the steepled roof and survey the surrounding area including, it is said, his barges making their way to the dock in Milton Creek at high tide.

LOOKING SOUTH UP PARK ROAD which, in Edwardian Sittingbourne, must have been regarded as very modern with its fine houses and wide thoroughfare. If potential motor traffic was in mind when the road was laid out, it was unfortunate that thought was not given to parking vehicles not in use. This open aspect can never be seen today without lines of cars necessarily being parked in the roadway. Many of the cast-iron railings and gates of the houses went the way of thousands of tons of such things in the Second World War when they were scrapped for the war effort.

MUCH HAS CHANGED HERE SINCE 1900, although there are a few buildings still recognizable in this view of East Street and Canterbury Road. The most striking difference is the roundabout at the junction of South Avenue. Some buildings have gone to make way for this, but on the left can be seen the protruding building of eighteenth-century date at No. 151 (used as butcher's premises for many years until recently) which is now a corner site on the roundabout. Further back towards the camera is the United Methodist Church (now Sittingbourne Sports Centre). Nearer still can be seen the old Sittingbourne Co-operative Society premises (see page 112 top). Walking and cycling are the only means of travel to be seen in this picture and the group of young people are outside shop premises which have survived. The tall building was the Co-op butchery (No. 88) and beyond that was the Wheatsheaf Inn. Many of the further houses, where South Avenue now joins East Street, have been demolished. In the distance the road rises to Snipeshill and was altogether more narrow and peaceful looking than seems possible today.

LOOKING WESTWARDS back along East Street, the house that formerly stood adjacent to the Wheatsheaf can just be seen on the left. A good view may also be had of the forecourt wall that used to stand in front of the Methodist Church, and the row of houses just beyond the Co-op site, where new Co-op premises are now (see page 112 top).

THIS VIEW OF CANTERBURY ROAD taken in around 1920 shows how smart the row of villas looked on the north side. Their iron railings and gates have unfortunately been lost, removed for the same wartime purposes alluded to earlier. The precise location can be determined by examining the large house behind the horse and delivery cart. The house remains together with the monkey-puzzle tree to the left which now stands considerably higher than the house.

SWANSTREE LODGE between Gaze Hill Avenue and Rectory Road is seen here at the turn of the century. The house was built for Mr Frank Peters (brother of Hedley Peters sen., page 121 et al.) who also had the flagpole erected for the purpose of flying the national flag on all ceremonial occasions and any other day when there seemed sufficient excuse. The rural surroundings have been lost, although a playing field still borders the grounds at the back of the house. Later dwellings now mask the front.

AT THE BOTTOM (N. END) OF WHAT IS NOW GORE COURT ROAD, stands this house, named 'Gortanore'. Photographed soon after it was built, the house was backed by fields and orchards. The new owners sat outside partaking of refreshment while the photographer set up his tripod in the field opposite. The occupant in 1908 was Richard William Cowper.

TO EMPHASIZE just how near the real countryside came to the town earlier this century this was part of the well-used Love Lane (now Park Drive) which led on southwards from the area of the house on the preceding page. It would be entertaining indeed if we could project back another 70/80 years before that, i.e., to around 1840, to see Sittingbourne before the development of paper and brickmaking etc., and glimpse the rural nature of the area then.

AMONG OTHER LARGE NOTABLE HOUSES appearing as a result of the new industrial prosperity of the town was The Limes, seen here from the back. It stood where London Road Trading Estate is now situated.

Schamel, Sittingbourne.

AT THE BOTTOM OF PARK ROAD the house fronting the convent school was known as 'Schamel'. This picture was taken 80 years ago and the house is strikingly similar in appearance today, although there have been subtle alterations to the porch and other features. The wide angle of the lens used by the photographer also deceptively altered the perspective and made the building appear wider than it actually is.

THE ATTRACTIVE ST MICHAEL'S MISSION ROOM, pictured here in around 1910, formerly stood in Canterbury Road, roughly opposite Bayford Road. The Mission Room was used as a school on weekdays and for worship on Sundays when a partition was raised on pulleys to reveal the altar. There was a separate vicar from that of St Michael's Church but the same curate served both.

THE OUTLYING VILLAGE OF HARTLIP to the west of Sittingbourne continues to be notable for its large and expensive houses. This is a postcard view of Parsonage House as seen from the north in around 1910. Adherence to traditional styles of architecture may be seen in features such as tile-hung walls and the semblance of timber-framing in the gable ends.

A NUMBER OF AERIAL PHOTOGRAPHS were taken of Sittingbourne and Kemsley paper mills in the 1920s. There are a number of striking differences that are apparent when comparing the town of today with this photograph which includes much of the central and north-west portion. The railway station near the bottom of the illustration still had a single span of roof covering the three platforms and beyond can be seen the houses demolished in recent years in the Princes Street and Eastbourne Street areas. There are also brickfields and, of course, an overall view of the mill. The station forecourt, St Michael's Road and The Forum Shopping Centre now comprise an area that has changed dramatically, much of it in the last 20 years. Note should be taken of the open spaces and fields to be seen at the top of the picture i.e., the west part of town beyond Chalkwell Road and towards Milton.

ON THE SOUTH SIDE OF TOWN lies King George's Playing Field bounded by Woodstock Road and Park Drive (see page 29). This area was part of the grounds of Gore Court, built by Gabriel Harper in the 1790s as a replacement for an earlier house which he had demolished. This view of the south front of the house dates from around 1885 and illustrates the six handsome columns which supported the portico. The large greenhouse/conservatory abutting the east side of the building appears to have been a replacement for one known to have existed there in 1838.

THIS VIEW OF GORE COURT HOUSE AND GROUNDS in 1905 again emphasises the extent to which bucolic countryside approached the town environs, and indeed at this time there were many more fields and orchards on the approaches to the main part of town. In the later nineteenth century Gore Court was owned by George Smeed until his death in 1881. His activities in brickmaking, cement manufacture and barge building had contributed much to the development of Sittingbourne.

ASh & Son.   R.A.M.C. Home Counties, pitching Tents at Gore Court Sittingbourne.

THE GROUNDS OF GORE COURT were used by the Territorial Force for annual training camps and, during the First World War, the house itself was also used by the army. Some would say misused for the condition of the building when vacated by the military might have caused conjecture as to whether part of the war had actually been fought within. In 1926 the house was demolished and a portion of the grounds were opened as a public park in 1937. The stable block remains, converted for use as a sports pavilion and the bases of some of the stone columns that formerly graced the front of the house still stand. This picture shows the Home Counties Unit of the Royal Army Medical Corps pitching their tents before the south front of the house.

VIEW IN GORE COURT PARK, early 1900s. The terraced houses of Sittingbourne's Park Road can just be seen advancing from the right in this view of the meeting of country and town. The break up of the Gore Court estate after the First World War led to extensive housing development in the former park. The lodge seen here is now No. 6 Gore Court Road on the corner of Bradley Drive.

WOOD COURT, GORE COURT. The rural character of Gore Court Park, just before the housing development, is emphasized in this photograph probably taken in the 1920s. The construction of houses in the Park Drive (Love Lane) area effectively carried Sittingbourne to the borders of Tunstall. Wood Court is now No. 1 Park Avenue, opposite the north entrance to King George's playing field.

MILTON, FROM LLOYD'S SHAFT.

THE PAPERMAKING MILLS OF EDWARD LLOYD LTD. (NOW BOWATERS) had a new and enormous chimney built in around 1901. This was known as 'Lloyds shaft' and in addition to dispersing smoke it provided, on at least one occasion, an ideal if precarious perch for an intrepid photographer. This north-east view from the top of the shaft in around 1905 overlooks Milton with, in the foreground, the large house occupied by the mill manager Mr T.T. Denson until it was demolished to make way for further mill extensions.

THE HIGH STREET OF MILTON REGIS, in this postcard view from the beginning of the century, presents an attractive period picture even though everyone present appears to have been pre-positioned and told to 'watch the birdie'. Without exception, push, pull and walk provided the only means of travel. At this time the population of Milton was about 7,000, having trebled in 50 years in accordance with the growth of many English towns (including Sittingbourne itself) during that period of rapid industrial growth. Milton had formerly been larger and more important than Sittingbourne, having been favoured by the Saxon kings. The modern town of Sittingbourne however has outstripped its older neighbour and encompasses it within its own boundaries. This view of Milton High Street shows many old buildings that remain today.

NORTH OF MILTON the new village of Kemsley was built in the 1930s to house workers at the new Kemsley papermaking mill. One hundred and eighty houses were finished by 1927 with a planned total of 750. A halt was provided on the railway line linking Sittingbourne and Sheerness, and a hall built for the leisure and social use of residents. Formerly separated from Milton by open fields, these are now being filled with extensive housing estates.

SECTION TWO

Creek, Commerce, Paper and Bricks

PAPERMAKING MACHINERY in the *Daily Chronicle* paper mills of Edward Lloyd. He was attracted to Sittingbourne by the freely available supply of water and moved his business from Bow in East London in the 1880s. Frank Lloyd followed his father in the firm until his death in 1927 when it was sold to Allied Newspapers. The mills were acquired by Bowaters in 1936.

THE GREAT FROST OF 1895 caused large ice floes to form in the creeks of the north Kent coast. In this photograph a line of barges are seen making their way along a channel in the ice in Milton Creek. An impressive indication of the massiveness of some of the ice blocks along the north Kent shore at that time may also be seen in one of the illustrations in the companion volume on Faversham.

THE MILTON CREEK CONSERVANCY ACT was passed in parliament in 1899 in order to serve the interests of creek users. A Conservancy Board was formed with representatives from shipowners, wharfingers, the County Council, the Councils of Sittingbourne, Milton Regis and single representative from the Admiralty. The moored barges in this picture of around 1905 are very heavily laden in contrast with the empty vessel departing on the full tide.

Bottom, left.
THIS PICTURE OF SAILMAKERS at Sittingbourne was taken between 1880 and 1885 and has an unmistakably foreman-like figure in the centre with bowler atop his no-nonsense rotund visage and a watch chain across his corpulent midriff. Next to him stands a bewhiskered army sergeant with pillbox hat. We do not know whether he was present at some special occasion or perhaps he simply joined in the group to have his picture taken. A surviving indenture reveals that in 1873 a seven-year apprenticeship was served by those wishing to become sailmakers.

BARGES MOORED ON MILTON CREEK at the beginning of the First World War waiting to unload at the nearby wharf. An optimistic guidebook in Edwardian times talked enthusiastically of the possibility of Milton Creek becoming a second Clyde. Although that prophetic wish has not so far materialized, any derisory laughter should perhaps be dampened down in the present climate of almost daily proposals of schemes for the dissection of Kent through 'development'.

THE CREEK at its most unphotogenic self at low tide, revealing the awesome mud which fortunately cannot be smelt through the medium of this picture. However, it evidently held no terrors for the two men on the left apparently digging for bait. The lighters on the right are being loaded with rolls of paper from the mill, subsequent to being towed by steam tug to London for the newspaper industry.

UNLOADING BALES OF PULP at the papermill wharf. The vast wall on the right is constructed from bales prepared in Scandinavia from timber felled there. The bales were shipped to Queenborough and transferred to lighters for towing into Milton Creek. The smaller crane could only have been used at this time to load finished rolls of paper from the rail trucks to the wharfside barge for lighterage to London, since its jib arm could not have reached to the top of the bale stacks.

THE HUGE STACKS OF WOODPULP AND PAPER WASTE were, and still are, a feature of the landscape beyond Kemsley. The enormous cranes uses for loading and unloading ran on tracks and, should one be unseated in a gale, the resulting catastrophe can be judged from this photograph showing many tons of machinery wedged in a gully.

LLOYDS MILL at Sittingbourne showing part of the office building and adjacent mill. The easy access to water and rail may be seen here with flatbed rail wagons alongside the mill building and in the process of being unloaded by the crane on an upper level. The bales of wood-pulp were conveyed by the mill's own light railway on wagons running from Sittingbourne to Kemsley where barges unloaded the material at the Company's wharves. The railway today is run as a private venture for pleasure purposes and is open to the public at frequent times.

A WIDER VIEW OF THE MILL OFFICES with two open touring type cars outside the main entrance. This postcard was sent on 18 November 1918 – a week after the armistice was signed to bring to an end the slaughter of the First World War. The sender of the card referred to the picture saying ' . . . here is the place where I shall soon be now all well again at home . . . '. Many Sittingbourne men lost their lives in the First World War and the trees and the plaques of The Avenue of Remembrance record their names. For others who survived, great relief must have been felt in returning to life and work at the mill and other employment around the town. In 1921, on the occasion of a visit by the Duke of York to Sittingbourne (see page 54), 333 employees at the mill formed a guard of honour in front of the works. All had served in the war.

IN THE EARLY YEARS OF THIS CENTURY the papermaking business of Edward Lloyd Ltd. employed nearly a thousand people, being at that time the largest paper mill in Great Britain. The premises were subsequently enlarged even further, the manager's large house being demolished to make way for the expansion. This picture of the offices and part of the mill in around 1900 also illustrates the use of horse-drawn wagons at the time.

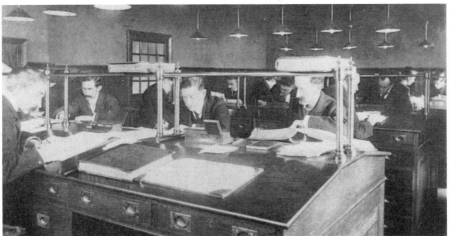

THE GENERAL OFFICE OF THE PAPER MILL in 1902 seems far removed from our conception of computer-equipped offices today which are also usually far more comfortably furnished. In fact this type of office lasted in many industrial firms until at least 1950. High and hard-seated stools were provided for an army of clerks making entries in the ledgers on brass-railed desks of solid mahogany. Hours were long, the work tedious, but life as a millhand would certainly not have appeared more attractive.

LLOYD'S MILL fulfilled contracts for the supply of paper to Australia and other overseas countries in addition to producing all the paper for the production of the *Daily Chronicle*. A good impression of working conditions within the mill in the early 1900s is provided by the photographs on this page. This picture is of the Reeling Room in the 'new mill'.

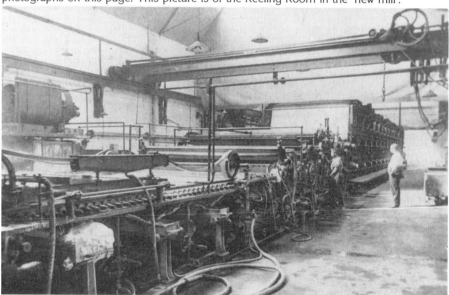

ENTITLED 'No.11 machine (wet end)' this illustration, again of around 1905, shows an enormous papermaking machine. In common with the interior view above, a striking impression is given of the potential hazards to be encountered in the working area. What would a factory inspector of today make of the unguarded drive belts and moving machinery, the cluttered floor space and meagre hand rails where they existed at all?

IN THE SERIES OF AERIAL VIEWS of the 1920s (see page 32) a fascinating comparison may be made using a modern street map and personal knowledge of the town today. In the top left-hand corner can be seen part of the Avenue of Remembrance laid out a few years previously. The railway line is clearly seen across the top of the scene, with the station forecourt and St Michael's Road to High Street area now almost completely different and developed. However, Station Street can be easily identified with Park Road beyond that. Nearer the centre were brick drying sheds, the paper mill and the head of the creek at low tide with a number of lighters alongside the wharf. On the far side there was still an orchard between Charlotte Street and Chalkwell Road.

A CLOSER VIEW of the centre portion of the previous illustration just includes West Street at the top of the picture with the bottom ends of William Street, Ufton Lane and Rock Road. Hawthorn Road connects with a footbridge over the railway, top right, to Charlotte Street. The head of the creek is just out of view (centre bottom) but the light railway and bridge connecting with the mill can be clearly seen as can some of the former houses which stood in the adjacent New Road and Lloyd Street. Near the fork of Mill Way and Church Street one or two of the old properties still remain.

THE NEWLY CONSTRUCTED KEMSLEY PAPER MILL, showing, top centre, Ridham Dock with connecting line to the mill and the massive coned heaps of material for conversion to paper. Top left is the old Kingsferry Bridge across The Swale connecting The Isle of Sheppey with the mainland. At the bottom right can be seen Milton Creek entering The Swale. The road approaching the mill from the left passed through the new village of Kemsley constructed for the workers at the mill (see page 38).

THE ROAD AND RAIL LINK with Sheppey across The Swale was at last rebuilt in 1960 when it was opened by the Duchess of Kent. At the same time the Old Ferry Road was also straightened and widened. The old bridge can be seen here, dwarfed by the nearly-completed lifting bridge which itself has now become inadequate to meet the pressure of traffic. An additional link with the island is now being proposed and will undoubtedly be needed if suggested development on Sheppey and at Ridham Dock reaches fruition.

THE WATERWORKS AT HIGHSTED was established in 1904 for the Milton Regis Urban District Council as it was then constituted. The cost was £14,680, to which Sittingbourne Urban Council contributed £6,000. The undertaking included the construction of the reservoir with a capacity of 550,000 gallons at the top of Stocker's Hill. This photograph, taken at the opening of the works, also shows the hill to the south-east almost as bereft of trees as it is now. In the interim period of course a fine beech wood developed, until the 1987 October storm virtually cleared the site.

THE SITTINGBOURNE CO-OPERATIVE SOCIETY opened their new bakery in St Michaels Road in 1937 when it was regarded as 'the most up to date in the South of England'. Entirely gas-fired it was initially very successful and the production of wrapped bread was very popular, '... in course of time it is anticipated that all bread sold will have to be wrapped, otherwise the hygienic methods of production and general cleanliness of the Bakery is nullified by unwrapped distribution'. The 'course of time' has shown that wrapped and unwrapped bread continued to be sold, it has also seen the demise of this particular bakery – it was demolished quite recently and the site is now occupied by light industrial units.

IN CONTRAST TO THE NEW 1937 CO-OPERATIVE BAKERY which has now vanished, the old bakery, opened in 1905 in Murston at the junction of Church Road and Tonge Road, still stands. This was described as the Steam Bakery and was built after the Sittingbourne Co-operative Society had been established for nearly 30 years of steady growth and progress. The membership had climbed to over 2,000 from 112 in 1874, the year of founding (see page 111). The photograph reproduced here shows the opening ceremony of the steam bakery on 10 June 1905. The building is now used as a furniture warehouse.

AT THE TURN OF THE CENTURY the chief industry of the Sittingbourne district was brickmaking, the reported output being 130 million per year. Overlying brickearth was excavated from much of the area (resulting in much farmland today being lower than adjoining roads) and thousands of houses in rapidly growing London were constructed with Sittingbourne bricks. The industry continued, with fluctuating fortunes, for many years and has still not died out in north Kent.

THE FOUR PICTURES ON THESE TWO FACING PAGES show something of the visit of the Duke of York to the brick works of Messrs C. Burley on 14 July 1921. The line of employees drawn up here may well have been ex-servicemen of the First World War, as they were later in the day at Lloyds Paper Mill (see page 105), and the man nearest the camera was wearing an old First World War army tunic. The duke took an interest in the welfare of ex-servicemen and would have been saddened to know that just 18 years after this occasion he would be reigning as King George VI over his country as it entered into the second war with Germany.

AT BURLEY'S BRICK WORKS Mr W. Mills, an employee with 50-years service, was presented to the duke. Among the other people assembled on this occasion were Mr W.T. Burley on the far left with hat in hand and, to the right-hand side of the picture, Mr L.R.Burley, distinguished by the mark around his head seemingly caused by a crushingly tight hat. Nearer the centre, partly hidden by Mr Mills, is probably Mr G.W. Burley.

SOME OF THE BURDEN we continue to place on what we affectionately refer to as our 'royals', is evident in this picture of nearly 70 years ago, revealing the implicit pressure on the duke as he was conducted at speed through the brick works (see page 105 & 106).

THERE ARE TWO LARGE CONNECTED CHALK QUARRIES AT HIGHSTEAD, divided by Cromers Road which for some reason, has become 'the nursery slopes' for learner drivers. The road forges straight ahead and upwards with the land quarried away on either side to an immense depth. Chalk excavated here was made into a slurry for the manufacture of cement. Quarrying is no longer continued and the depths have been reclaimed in part by nature. It is a pity that imaginative use is not made of the quarries; nature reserves and recreational space seem obvious choices. Each would partly meet a neglected need amidst the insidious creep of development in the south-east.

Country Life and Work

Harvesting near Sittingbourne

g. ash.

FRUIT GROWING AND FARMING have a longer history than brick and papermaking in the development of Sittingbourne. The first English cherry orchard was established at Teynham in the reign of Henry VIII. Fruit growing has declined to some extent and the nature of orchards with closer compact trees and denuded ground has changed, but the district is still one of mixed fruit and arable farming. The sight of sheaves being stacked in stooks to dry is very rarely seen now, and usually only when a special wheat straw is required for thatch. In this picture of harvesting near Sittingbourne, probably in the 1920s, a three-horse team was working abreast.

THE MANSION OF WOODSTOCK, seen here in around 1900, formerly stood near Tunstall to the south of Sittingbourne. It was built in around 1780 and had a succession of owners, being regarded, for a period in the nineteenth century, as the family home of the Twopeny family. Of the latter, the most notable was William (1797–1873), whose time was divided between the family legal business and making drawings of architecture and antiquities. He was an accomplished draughtsman and 38 volumes of his drawings and notebooks are in the keeping of the British Museum. Woodstock lingered on until the 1960s, becoming a ruin used for civil defence training and finally being demolished. The site is a rise in the field opposite and to the north of the entrance to Shell Research Ltd.

Torry Hill.

THE PRESENT TORRY HILL HOUSE designed in an attractive style reminiscent of the mid-seventeenth century was built in 1957, being a replacement, delayed by the war, of the older and much bigger house demolished in 1937. The latter, which is pictured here, was a huge Victorian house built for Lord Kingsdown who put together the Torry Hill estate.

THIS PICTURE OF HALES HOUSE at Tunstall not only shows the historic Coffin Pond in good order, but also reveals a glimpse of open countryside behind the house where there are now roads and houses. Hales house was built in the first half of the seventeenth century for the Hales family. Soon after, England became torn by civil war with doubtless many alarms in Tunstall where some of the gentry were steadfast Royalists. In a later, but not unrelated upheaval, James II is believed to have taken refuge at Hales House, home of his friend Sir Edward Hales. It is certain that these walls, and those of Tunstall House nearby, have survived many unimaginable changes of fortune.

THESE COTTAGES IN TUNSTALL ROAD remain as they appeared in this picture of around 1920. On the right is now the opening to Cranbrook Drive and the new houses on part of the Old Gore Court estate. On the left, behind the white posts, there also remains a pond, severely constricted between the road and the hedge. This pond is of great age, being shown on Hasted's map of around 1780, as is Coffin Pond referred to above. Probably both are of much older age than that.

EAST OF TUNSTALL IS HIGHSTED where a junction of roads lies at the foot of Stocker's Hill leading to Rodmersham Green. On the extreme left of this picture is a glimpse of orchard where there is now an open field. However, the few trees seen here interestingly reveal the use of sticky fruit bands tied round the trunks. This evokes memories of orchards that commonly displayed this use of pest control which has now been replaced by the all-pervading insecticide spray.

Bridges Farm, Rodmersham Green.

IN THIS PICTURE OF BRIDGE'S FARM at Rodmersham Green some 50 years ago are seen other features evocative of a passing age. Oast-houses generally fell into disuse, until recently acquiring status akin to buried treasure for any farmer fortunate enough to own them. The current trend is to convert them into housing units for sale at remarkable prices. The spile and wire fencing seen here survives as a type in this area where chestnut coppicing is still a viable crop.

RODMERSHAM GREEN WINDMILL still had its sweeps and cap in 1910. Built of brick, this tower mill fell into disuse until, without its cap, the top was converted into an observation 'spotting' post in the Second World War. More recently it failed to survive the notice of developers and it was demolished to make way for a new house. The large commonland green survives however, still flanked by houses of various periods.

HERE AT BORDEN the 'unmade' nature of many country roads at the beginning of this century is clearly seen. It was then a rural community with a population of about 1,200 based on an agricultural economy of fruit, hops and corn. It is still a farming area, with the tentacles of Sittingbourne reaching out to it via Borden Lane, but as almost everywhere in the south-east the village is growing in size and serving as a 'dormitory' for nearby towns.

LOOKING BACK DOWN THE VILLAGE STREET of Borden from the tiny green near the church, the Maypole Inn can be seen on the left with a glimpse of the forge opposite which is still functioning. Out of view of the camera on the right (but seen in the distance in the previous illustration) still stands the attractive building built in 1823 by the trustees of William Barrow, who left property in 1707 to produce income for the benefit of 'widows and poor men' of Borden. The building has a fine upper-floor meeting room for the assemblage of those who still administer the charity.

THE ROAD AT BORDEN bends round the churchyard, the wall of which can be seen on the right. The church seen in the illustration at the foot of the previous page (see also page 157 top), is part Norman and contains a monument to Dr Robert Plot, an early historian who died in 1696 and lived at Sutton Baron in an outlying part of the parish. The area around the church seen here remains very picturesque, including the sixteenth-century timber-framed house opposite the church.

THERE ARE MANY FINE OLD HOUSES in the district and this picture of Queen Down Warren at Hartlip in 1909 shows an interesting example of good quality timber-framing in a house that has an unusual history. It was moved from a site closer to the village to its present situation in 1841. The date of 1566 above the door refers to the addition of the Elizabethan porch, a common practice at that time. The right-hand end looks of similar date, the left-hand end appears earlier, but with all that shifting around in 1841 it would be unwise to be adamant about it.

THE KEY INN formerly stood at the corner of the junction of London Road and King's Ferry Road with another road leading off to Detling and Maidstone. The eighteenth-century farmhouse fell to the bulldozer also. Now there is a huge roundabout with a new trunk road carved through the hillside and more is to come, for Sheerness Docks eject their container lorry tidal wave this way.

AT MILTON REGIS this photograph of Meads Mill was taken in around 1890. It shows the mill in use for grinding corn with two men and a fine Kentish wagon outside. A millstone leans against the octagonal brick base, constructed to give extra height to a mill in a low situation. The timber-framed superstructure was weather boarded to give the typical appearance of a 'smock' mill which once dotted our countryside in their hundreds. In 1908 John Bates, 'Corn, Hay, Seed Merchant and Miller', owned the mill and advertised his services to farmers and others for grinding, crushing or rolling corn. Meads Mill was sited at Mill Way and was demolished in around 1950. One of the millstones is set in the forecourt of the Court Hall museum.

THIS POSTCARD VIEW of a 'Wealden' type fifteenth-century hall-house at Milstead shows the building in use as a post office about 50 years ago. It has now reverted to private residential use and remains a very attractive example of its type with several interesting architectural features; the two-centred head of the front entrance and the wall-plate carried on arched braces across the face of the recessed hall may be seen here.

THIS LADY IN EDWARDIAN COSTUME stands at the gate of the house featured in the previous illustration. The central part of this enviable and tranquil rural scene is occupied by Milstead church (see page 6). This photograph was taken in busier days as far as the churches were concerned. At a time when the parish population was scarely above 200, there were two services every Sunday in additon to communion, plus a children's service, plus Sunday School. There was an additional communion once a month, matins every day and a special prayer service on Fridays.

JOHN BATES WAS THE MILLER at Mede Mill in Milton Regis in 1908. Unlike the similar view below, this scene has not endured. The mill once stood at the bottom of Lower Mede in Vicarage Road where the changing rooms are now sited. The pond has gone but there are traces of old brickwork in a hedge.

TONGE MILL seen across the well-filled millpond which lies below the remains of a motte and bailey. It is believed that the site was occupied by Saxon settlers even earlier. The mill buildings of course are of an age much nearer to our own, the tallest built in local brick in 1837, and across the road behind the tall chimney, the millhouse of 1759 clad in weather-board adopts an inebriated posture as it staggers back from the road. This attractive view remains remarkably similar today.

GREENSTREET IN AROUND 1910 looking towards Faversham with the George Inn (page 117 bottom) on the right-hand side of the road, properly part of Lynsted. Just beyond is Lynsted Lane eventually leading to Doddington. Opposite is the tall Co-op building (see page 134) now replaced by a modern shop. Half in Teynham, half in Lynsted, called Greenstreet, the locals have it sorted out but most people now call the whole lot Teynham. Teynham is really on the north side of the road, towards the railway station, where it is called Barrow Green!

TEYNHAM WAS ONCE FAVOURED ENOUGH to have an archbishop's palace built there. That scourge of ecclesiastical self-aggrandisment, Henry VIII, still held Teynham in some regard, for his fruiterer, Richard Harrys, introduced hereabouts the first cherry orchards in the country. Some of the old rural aspect remains in Cellar Hill, seen here in 1904, with a peep of The Burrs built in 1901 behind the trees on the left and the presently named Tudor Cottage opposite.

REGARDLESS OF PLACE NAMES these chaps knew where they caught their rats. The box normally held the ferrets, but for this photograph in 1913 'Pop' Neaves, seated with bowler hat, held two ferrets, and seated on his right was the young Stan Ruck clutching another of the furry rat flushers. Standing, from left to right: Bert Ruck (holding an antique looking firearm), Cliff Randle and Amos Brown, each with double-barrelled twelve-bores and, finally, depicted unfortunately where the picture is badly creased, Bill Gates. Peering apprehensively from behind the legs of Amos Brown is a renowned rat-catching dog, perhaps anticipating the sudden escape of a giant rodent from beneath the photographer's black cloth?

THE PICTURESQUE COTTAGES at the Lynsted end of Ludgate Lane are seen here with the wall of the churchyard on the right. It is a beautiful spot where history abounds, the church survived bad bomb damage in the last war. It is worth visiting at any time, especially when the flower festival is in progress. Do not miss the marvellous monument to Lord Teynham of 1622 by Epiphanius Evesham.

LYNSTED COURT has stood empty but weathertight alone in a field for over 20 years. It is a large timber-framed house probably of various periods and not all as late as the Elizabethan exterior suggests. The right-hand end, beyond the porch, is almost an entity in itself, like an Elizabethan town house that has been lifted up and stuck on to the main structure.

IF YOU KNOW ANY CHERRY ORCHARDS, photograph and enjoy them while you may, they are disappearing fast. This photograph was taken in 1920 by Mr Ferris, leader of the fire brigade in Teynham (see page 133). He was a keen photographer and left us this splendid picture of cherry-picking, showing many items of interest that remained common until recently. The women all wore head coverings of some sort, with aprons or overalls. They evidently climbed the wide-footed fruit ladders with ease, gathering the cherries into the small baskets for emptying into the large round wicker baskets as shown at the foot of the centre ladder (cf. page 81). The man was Stan Ruck (see page 69).

DODDINGTON is on the southern edge of the area dealt with in this book. It is situated in the Newnham valley at the bottom of the extremely long climb to the top of the hill above Hollingbourne, complained of by William Cobbett in his *Rural Rides*. The village also marks the limit of the best orchards stretching down from Sittingbourne. To the south the land is poorer and more suitable for arable farming. This picture of the village street in the pre-kerbstone age, around 1914, shows the post office on the left with the postmaster Henry Allan Jarvis standing outside and his aproned son Allan in the shop doorway. A little further on is the butcher's (see page 75) past a lady in long dress and hat, and a man leading a horse. The Chequer's pub is in the distance and on the right is the Methodist Chapel now converted for use as the village hall.

THE NATURE OF THE UNMADE ROAD can clearly be seen in this view of Doddington Street looking west in around 1910. On the right is Yew Tree House, as it was then called, although now it is divided into cottages. It was originally built in around 1500 as a single farmhouse, and derives its present name from the large yew tree which still stands in the corner of the nearest front garden, despite some muttered threats in deference to the great god, motor car. The notice on the chimney stack advised the world that the occupant of the premises was Henry Elvy, 'Practical Gate-Maker and Spile Fencer'. An example of spile fencing, i.e., chestnut and wire, with the spiles driven into the ground, may be seen below Mr Elvy's notice, nearest the camera.

THREE MEN AND A DOG paused in Doddington while the photographer set up his tripod on the bank opposite what is now the recreation ground in the early 1900s. The gent supported on the shovel was perhaps the lengthsman, charged with keeping the road clean. On the far left the cottages of West End, with Dully Hill stretching up to the right, may be glimpsed. The surface of the latter is still 'unmade' and very probably in a worse state than it was when this picture was taken. The long white building facing the field served for a time as a workhouse. It has recently been demolished to make way for new housing.

NEARER THE FAVERSHAM (EASTERN) END of Doddington Street this picture, again in Edwardian times, depicts a number of buildings which no longer exist. The nearest cottage has long since gone, the next house was the School House where Thomas Potts the headmaster lived at about this time. It was an attractive late Georgian red-brick house with parapet all round, unnecessarily demolished by the county council in around 1969, a cracked wall providing the excuse. Further along was the forge of Cobb the blacksmith, beneath the low hipped roof, which was also demolished in the late 1960s.

JUSTIFIABLY FAMED beyond the local area this shop in Doddington is popularly referred to as 'Doughty's the butchers'. However, this early photograph predates the start of the Doughty era. At the beginning of this century the shop was owned by Sydney Boulding (see page 11), but was managed in 1908 by Ernest Jackson who lived in the adjoining house. It was very probably Mr Jackson who is featured here outside the shop. It has much the same appearance today, except that the meat is kept inside the shop or the cold room and not displayed outside as was the common practice then.

DODDINGTON as seen from the top of the hill adjoining Seed Road, formerly Hope's Hill. Seen here in around 1910 the skyline is dominated by Doddington windmill with, to the right, the large building which was known at different times as Stephenson's Convalescent Home, Highgate Wood Lodge and later The National Children's Home. It is now known as 'Southdowns', a children's home run by Kent County Council. In the village street Allan Jarvis is seen standing at the door of the post office and the Wesleyan Chapel may be glimpsed behind the large tree. The meadow in the foreground may have been used for fairs or similar gatherings 200-300 years ago, as coins of that period have occasionally been found there.

Right.
DODDINGTON WINDMILL was built in 1816. The date is still deeply and artistically inscribed with initials J & S, N, in the brickwork of the chimney-stack of the miller's cottage close by. The mill was of the Kentish 'smock' variety, constructed on a low brick and flint base, there being little need to seek extra height due to the exposed situation high above the village. This photograph was taken in 1903/4 and shows the miller and owner Mr Stanley Norrington with his dog Victor and holding his horse 'Gyp'. Mrs Norrington is holding her baby Frederick Douglas who only survived to the age of five. The gate marked the end of the Mill Lane, now a private drive, leading to Chequers Hill. The mill was demolished around the time of the Second World War having become derelict. A local builder paid £1 for the structure, sawed through the eight principal posts and pulled the whole over with a rope. The materials were sold off but the base remains and two millstones are also on the site.

OLD MILL COTTAGE , Doddington (see previous page) as it appeared in 1946, representing a basically similar appearance to that of 1816 when it was built, although the nearest end, as seen here, was a small addition. During the 1950s and early 1960s small extensions were added. Substantial alterations and additions were made, mainly in the 1970s, although the core of the original cottage remains.

DODDINGTON PLACE was built in 1870 with red bricks made locally on the estate. This picture shows the house before the addition of the present main front, which encloses a splendid reconstructed Jacobean panelled hall with gallery. The materials were brought down from the north and constitute an imposing interior to the otherwise uncertain architecture which hovers between Gothic Revival and Victorian in style. The house once had its own gasworks in the street, on the site of 'Whitemans', providing a private supply for the main house on the hill and certain smaller properties in the village before the arrival of the 'Company's gas'.

Sharsted Court.

SHARSTED COURT is also mentioned in the book in this series dealing with Faversham, for it is situated on the hill above the village of Newnham and is directly approached from the village street there. However, it properly lies within the parish of Doddington. The manor of Sharsted existed before 1174, the present huge and rambling house encompasses part, at least, of a building standing in 1374, and the Queen-Anne front of 1711 seen here was probably a modernizing facelift to the medieval house. There are still some enormously thick flint and chalk walls, indicating that some of the fabric is likely to represent portions of the house of John de Sharsted, i.e., mid-thirteenth century. In 1935 Elizabeth Selby appropriately described Sharsted as a beautiful example of an old English Manor House, which it still is. There also remains a large area of woodland in which a famous avenue of beeches existed until it was destroyed by the Forestry Commission after the last war in favour of regimented rows of firs. However, there is some intermixture of deciduous hardwood with these. The Commission recently decided they did not want it after all and the woodland has happily been acquired again by the Wade family who are the present owners of the Court. Canon and Mrs E.H. Wade, who bought the property over twenty years ago, much loved this wonderful old house and their descendants cherish it with care and understanding also.

THE FORMER YOUTH HOSTEL at Margaret Manor in the extreme south of the parish of Doddington provided the YHA with an isolated but popular hostel after they acquired it in around 1950. This building was part of the privately owned and run hospital/home of Dr Josiah Oldfield, later becoming a boys' home for East End lads. It is now a private residential home for the physically and mentally handicapped.

HOP GARDENS NEAR SITTINGBOURNE in 1896/1900. The system seen here was that of growing the hops on poles, which were carried to the bins for picking. Gradually superseded by the pole and wire system, where the bines were stripped from the wires and carried to the bins, the two methods remained in use for an overlapping period of many years. Essentially the picking, a type of hand labour drawn from local communities and London, remained constant for a century and more. In 1930, of 413 parishes in Kent, 335 grew hops. Mechanization now deals with picking the relatively few hop fields that remain.

THIS SITTINGBOURNE CHERRY ORCHARD of around 1900, reveals that the methods and baskets in use were identical to those of twenty years later (see page 71). Here, the scales for weighing the large baskets of fruit may be seen on the left of the picture. Regrettably no identities are known of the pickers here, but it may be seen that their life was 'fruitful' in more than one sense. There were nine small children among the ten ladies, of whom one at least was pregnant. Motherhood was no bar to this type of work, the orchards in fine weather provided an ideal playground for the children. There are still a few cherry orchards like this one covered with grass. The ground in many modern apple orchards is regularly sprayed with herbicide, any blade of grass that dares to show a tentative green shoot receives short shrift. The finer particles of soil and organic matter are leached out of the bare soil and washed away by heavy rains. Worms will not find the ground hospitable or abundant in food, and without them the soil structure becomes compacted until the orchard cannot produce economic returns and the whole lot is grubbed out to start again, or perhaps to be used for growing grain.

ANY CHAPTER CONCERNED WITH COUNTRY LIFE, should properly include a representative or two of the village churches which have played such a large part in the life of the communities which they serve. Frinsted Church, seen here with an Edwardian lady at the churchyard gate with its wrought-iron arch and lamp bracket, must have had reeling sensibilities after the rampaging restorations of its Victorian keepers. However, many features of the earlier periods remain and time, together with the devotions of the faithful over centuries, imbues all with the awesome peace and serenity of the English country church.

WORMSHILL is a rural neighbour of Frinsted up on the high ground. This hamlet has survived without growing much in size for a thousand years. Portions of the church are possibly late Saxon with the main part from the thirteenth century. It too survived another of those Victorian onslaughts, but will the Church generally and such rural hamlets as this, survive the incomprehensible changes of this century's end?

SECTION FOUR

Road Transport

ANYTHING ILLUSTRATING TRANSPORT over seventy years ago should first emphasise legs as being the prime mover in transporting people about. There is no doubt that walking was the main way of getting to work and going about day-to-day business. However, most people would still not categorize the lower members of the body as transport. So, having made the point, the first picture selected shows the next most popular means of locomotion: cycling. This was taken at Bredgar in 1907 and titled 'Auntie Edie on her bicycle'.

THIS PHOTOGRAPH OF STYLE'S THREE SQUIRRELS INN at Stockbury on the Maidstone road was taken by Mr Ramell in around 1900. He thoughtfully arranged three kinds of horse-drawn transport outside, thus providing for us the main points of interest. Mr Ongley's three-horse bus had inside protection for most passengers on the long and often bad-weather haul over Detling Hill. There was room outside for luggage together with the more hardy and hard-up passengers. The conveyance on the left with a pair of horses is rather indistinct but appears to be another bus with several parcels on top. No doubt the opportunity would be taken to use the regular trips between the towns for the carriage of small parcels and packets. In the centre of the picture is two-wheeled chaise drawn by a grey. The Three Squirrels made an ideal staging point on a sometimes arduous journey.

MOTOR BUSES were coming into common use by the First World War. Many of the London buses were commandeered to move the troops around in wartime France. Soon after the end of the war the first bus to regularly trundle up and down the present A2 (see page 88), carried passengers into Sittingbourne from Teynham and intermediate points and in fact made the trip from Faversham to Maidstone.

MR E. W. BUSHELL chauffeured the first car owned by Lloyds papermill. It was a Rolls-Royce and is seen here in around 1912. The array of highly-polished lamps would alone be the envy of any vintage car enthusiast today. Mr Bushell had formerly worked in the garage of W.J. Pullen at the bottom of Park Road, who had supplied the vehicle to Lloyds.

High Street, Sittingbourne.

T. Ash & Sons.

SITTINGBOURNE HIGH STREET in 1909, with the town hall clock on the left and Fletcher's butchers on the right, had not a motor vehicle in sight. There were many bicycles parked by the kerb and several horse-drawn conveyances, some delivering goods to the shops, but also some evidently of private ownership including the pony and the trap on the right. To be noted are the sun blinds on the north side of the street, which generally seem to have reached further across the pavement than any modern counterpart does, and it can be imagined that our present commercial traffic would certainly collide with some of these extended blinds if they were in use today.

THIS SIMILAR VIEWPOINT in Sittingbourne High Street in the 1950s, contrasts sharply, in the nature of the traffic, with the view on the facing page taken over forty years earlier. Ponies and traps have gone in favour of private saloon motor cars, while the British Road Services Austin lorry facing towards the camera was the delivery vehicle of the day. Nearer, on the right, can be seen the golden grasshopper sign of Martin's Bank, and the inn sign of The Lion where a garage with cars for hire and petrol were all available. Taxis were also obtainable there. Nearer still, a Belisha Beacon marked the spot were pedestrians could try their luck at the increasingly hazardous sport of road crossing.

THIS VIEW OF THE FIRST MOTOR BUS SERVICE (see page 85) between Faversham and Sittingbourne reveals many further interesting details. Parked outside The George Inn at Greenstreet (see page 117) the solid-tyred bus bears the name 'Straker and Squire' on the radiator. It had one large headlamp, apparently electric. The driver's cab was open, as was the stairway enabling passengers to reach the top or outside. Chocks were available to place under the wheels to assist braking and stability on slopes. The registration number on the vehicle was KT 613, a number denoting the early provenance of the vehicle, and one that would be coveted by collectors today. The driver and conductor were uniformed, and the driver was able to use the splendid curved and manually operated horn by his right shoulder to give warning of his approach, or in this case perhaps, warning of the imminent capsizing due to overloading on top.

MR WALLY PULLEN, owner of the garage at the bottom of Park Road in Sittingbourne (see page 24 bottom) was an inventive man. He stands here, felt-hatted, 'Albert'-chained and smoking a pipe, on the right-hand side regarding with satisfaction the car which he had converted to a mobile sawbench, using the engine of the vehicle to power the sawblade. To his right stood the bareheaded Mr Southall, owner of the ground at Tunstall where the logs were being cut up. (Mr Southall built the bungalow in Tunstall Road near the top of Cranbrook Drive.) Mr Pullen's brother was operating the saw. Next on the left was Mr E.W. Bushall (see page 85), wearing a chauffeur's-cap, splitting logs. On the far left is the blurred image of an unidentified soldier probably on leave during the First World War, assisting in the log-splitting task. The car is believed to have been a Rover, the battered number plate appears to read D431. The vehicle was evidently jacked up and supported under the rear axle on triangular chocks. The saw was not in motion when the photograph was taken, and it remains uncertain whether the rear wheels would turn clear of the ground when the saw was in use.

SECTION FIVE

Events, Celebrations and War

THE CORONATION OF KING GEORGE V in 1911 was marked by local demonstrations of loyalty everywhere, in the days when patriotism was proudly displayed whenever the chance was available. In Park Road the photographer had an audience that included a few of the men that evidently were responsible for the flags and bunting. Seen here outside Shepherd Neame's Park Tavern the group included a very tall man in a trilby hat, but otherwise dressed as though for a cricket match.

THE SITTINGBOURNE BAPTIST TABERNACLE annual outing made its way up Canterbury Road past the opening to Harold Road and Terrace road on the way to the Rectory playing fields in this photograph of around 1900. The ground on the left was still used for allotments on Gay's Hill Field (now Gaze Hill Road) and the footpath on that side had no kerb. As the procession approached the junction of Murston Road it had reached the edge of town at that time. The outings were very popular, there are at least fifteen farm waggons to be seen here and over two hundred people taking part.

Right.
THIS FINE VIEW of Sittingbourne High Street was probably taken from the top of the Georgian building at Nos. 59 and 61, formerly occupied by Henry S. Tett & Co., ironmongers and agricultural engineers. The procession was for Lifeboat Day, probably in 1904 (see pages 96 and 97 top). The leading float carried figures gaily costumed, apparently in the guise of Britannia. A group of sea cadets came next, followed by a long procession stretching back past St Michael's Church well into East Street. The picture reveals by the roofs and old facades how many period buildings existed in this central part of the town. Several have gone and it is regrettable that, with few exceptions, the remainder have not received sympathetic treatment to show them at their best.

SITTINGBOURNE CO-OPERATIVE SOCIETY'S ANNUAL DEMONSTRATION is shown on these two facing pages (see page 90) moving past the Baptist Tabernacle, probably in around 1906. The Baptist Church marked the end of the High Street and the beginning of West Street. The first shop to be seen here bore the name Webb at No. 3, Ebenezer Blackman dealt in greengrocery at No. 3A and next door at No. 5 and 7 was Percy Charles Hubbard, saddler, harness maker and boot salesman ('... Wear Hubbard's Boots ...'). The occupants of these shops took the chance to see the procession from the ideal vantage point of their upstairs windows. The next building on the south side was Bourne House and then the wall of the Police Station can just be glimpsed in the picture on the next page.

THESE TWO PICTURES of the same procession provide a rewarding study of the fashions of the day. The cloth cap, recognised symbol of the working man for decades, may be seen on the heads of the onlookers. The same headgear was worn by a woman with a shawl near the bottom left-hand corner of this picture. To her right were two women wearing clothes nearer to our present conception of the attire of 'Edwardian Ladies'; picture hats, long dresses and gloves. The baby carried by one looks finely dressed too. Even further to the right there walked an elderly lady at the edge of the procession, showing us that some older people retained the fashion of the previous age; her appearance is nearer Victorian. In the same vein, consider the old gentleman standing at the edge of the kerb on the left. He had a soft hat, white beard and stick by his side, again Victorian in appearance and contrasting with the straw boaters and bright dress of the young people.

ON LIFEBOAT SATURDAY in 1904 the parade was led by the Fire Officer, Hedley Peters, who will be mentioned again later. Behind came a police band followed by a contingent of soldiers with rifles at the slope. They were marching down Park Road and small boys at the front carried collecting boxes inviting donations from the onlookers for the lifeboat fund. Interestingly, at the junction with West Street at the bottom of the picture, can be seen the cobbled crossing for pedestrians crossing Park Road between the footpaths on either side. On the left can be seen part of the old police station, now the magistrates court. On the right the ivy-covered building was well-known for several years as Pullen's Garage, it was bombed in the Second World War and a vacant plot remains there still.

HEDLEY PETERS ASTRIDE HIS HORSE appeared to be establishing several lengths lead over the police band, as he led the procession on almost certainly the same occasion as that on the previous page. A delightful cameo within the main picture is that of the young lady and her sailor escort. Her dress is essentially Edwardian and the sailor's uniform basically remained the same for well over half a century.

SITTINGBOURNE FIRE BRIGADE acquired a new horse-drawn steam fire engine on 8 June 1898 (see pages 121 and 122). To mark the occasion a display and parade was mounted by the brigades from Rochester, Chatham, Faversham, Milton and Sittingbourne.They are seen here assembled, together with a large crowd on the old forecourt of Sittingbourne railway station. There is added interest in the details of the buildings, some of which have now disappeared.

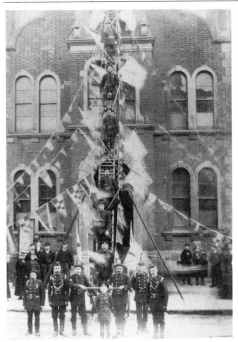

IN AN ERA when Sittingbourne Fire Brigade played a prominent part in the life of the town through their participation in parades, processions etc. (see separate section) no opportunity was lost to display and demonstrate their equipment. In 1899 the team set up their new escape ladder before the old Town Hall. With the ladder suitably bedecked with bunting and flags, and with their young mascot (Hedley Peters jun., later to succeed his father as Chief Officer of the brigade) the team proudly posed for this photograph.

THE FIRST WORLD WAR of 1914–18 brought the first experiences of aerial bombing to the British public, to whom war had previously been an undertaking that its largely victorious armies had for many years conducted overseas. The First World War changed the world in many ways, for the people of Sittingbourne who were beginning to lose their sons in the fields of France, the Zeppelin airship raids were a new horror. This crowd of sightseers in Unity Street were looking at the damage to the back of houses in Park Road (St Mary's Church is on the left) after the Zeppelin raid of 4 June 1915. What would their thoughts have been if they had known that a short 25 years later the populations of many British cities would be subjected to harrowing scenes of far worse devastation? Under the Defence of the Realm Act of 1914 it was supposedly illegal to take photographs of such scenes,

Bottom, left.

THE HOME OF MR HEDLEY PETERS (auctioneer, valuer, estate and emigration agent, and enthusiastic captain of the fire brigade) at No. 93 High Street was impressively decorated on 22 June 1911 for the coronation of King George V, whose portrait, with that of his Queen, was displayed with the Union Jack flags. Also prominent was the double portrait of the old King, Edward VII and Queen Alexandra, and the Prince of Wales' feathers to mark the former title of both kings. Number 93 has remained in continuous use for the business of estate valuation and agency up to the present time.

THE UNITY STREET and Park Road bomb damage caused by the Zeppelin raid of 4 June 1915 is referred to on the previous page. This shows wondering onlookers regarding the damage to the front of the houses, some of which already had their shattered windows boarded up. A strangely incongruous note is struck by the straw-hatted man in the foreground who, amidst the scene of violence and devastation, carried a small sunshade to protect himself from the early June sun.

MANY PICTURES TAKEN BY W. HARGRAVE, a redoubtable and tireless professional photographer whose business premises were in Preston Street, Faversham, are featured in the companion volume to this book, *Faversham In Old Photographs*. Mr Hargrave made haste to Sittingbourne after the Zeppelin raid, despite the official regulations (see previous page). In this picture and the following page he captured something of the worried and concerned mood of the onlookers. The bomb exploded on top of a garden wall and the only casualty was said to be a blackbird.

THE TWO HARGRAVE PHOTOGRAPHS of the Zeppelin bomb damage in June 1915 are misdated 'July 1916'. They are without doubt the scenes following the June 1915 raid. Could the wrong date be some means by which Mr Hargrave avoided contravention of the 1914 Act alluded to on page 99? Or perhaps he did not publish the pictures until after the war, by which time he may have inadvertently mistaken the date. Newspapers of the time carried no pictures or reports of the events.

DONALD DEAN BEING WELCOMED HOME by the citizens of Sittingbourne after he was awarded the Victoria Cross for bravery in France. The white-bearded figure on the right of the platform was George Dean, Donald's grandfather.

THE ROYAL WEST KENT REGIMENT were billeted at Gore Court Park (now King George V playing field) in 1916; recovering and re-forming after a period of fighting in France. It is said that at Ypres the regiment was in the trenches when Hill 60 was mined. A call went out for all the men to follow a surviving officer and there were seven men able to respond to the call. In Sittingbourne the regiment recruited many men and the names of some are commemorated in the Avenue of Remembrance. The recruiting parade seen here was passing up West Street towards the High Street. William Street is on the left with the business of Frank Hadlow on the corner.

ANOTHER RECRUITING PARADE of the Royal West Kent Regiment in 1916 with their band leading the column marching up West Street. On the left were two milk carts belonging to A.S. Fowler outside the West End Creameries. The horse-drawn float reminds us of the days when milk was sold in the street and dipped from the open churn. The horse incidently was too busy with his nose in the chaff box to be aware of how fortunate he was not to have been drafted to France. In June 1916 the first Military Service Act was passed in parliament introducing the first compulsory service for men. After being attested men were conscripted to the army if they were fit and met other conditions of age etc. Exemption could be applied for. A Doddington farmhand who milked cows and also had his own smallholding was reluctantly granted exemption from June until Michaelmas. The Tribunal said that women would have to do that type of work. A Lynsted huntsman who looked after the horses of the Tickham Hunt was granted exemption after letters were read to the Tribunal stating the importance of maintaining hunts and riding facilities thus afforded to officers.

MEASURES TAKEN during the First World War years became ever more stringent and costly until, by 1918, the cost to the nation was over £6,000,000 per day. To assist in the financing of this, the Goverment issued war bonds. Nation-wide efforts were made to publicize and sell the loan stock. In Sittingbourne this photograph of such an occasion was taken from the upstairs window of No. 93 High Street (see page 98 bottom), looking east. The banner strung across the road from the town hall read 'Buy Your War Loan here Today' and the packed crowd included many service personnel. The buildings opposite include a number that no longer exist and the site is partly occupied by the large building later erected for Burtons the tailors.

THE FIRST WORLD WAR was over in 1921, although the effects were such that the world would never be the same again and an era had truly ended. However, the young Duke of York looked to the future of his country as did his brother Edward (although the duke was not to know at this stage that he would succeed his brother as sovereign fifteen years later). The duke visited Sittingbourne (see page 54 and 55) on 14 July 1921 for a whirlwind tour of farms and industry which commenced at Rainham. On the way to Sittingbourne he was cheered by fruit pickers and schoolchildren, and at the town hall he visited a sale of work and a garden fête raising money for disabled soldiers. Other events of the day included visiting brick works, the paper mills, a jam factory and a cherry orchard (see also the following page).

THE PHOTOGRAPHS on this and the preceding page are scenes at 'Whitehall' in Bell Road, the residence of Mr G.H. Dean whose grandson was Captain Donald Dean VC (see page 101 bottom), where the Duke took lunch on the day of his visit in 1921. On page 105 he is seen seated on the steps of the house near the conservatory. The various other persons present include Mrs (later to become lady) Loetitia Olympia Honeyball, Mr and Mrs Dean and Mr Frank Lloyd. The picture on this page shows the duke leaving 'Whitehall' after his visit, with Mr Lloyd standing next to the car and Mr Dean in conversation to the rear. Seated next to the chauffeur was wing commander Craig who was in close attendance to the duke throughout his visit.

THE DUKE OF KENT journeyed between official visits in an open tourer on his visit to Sittingbourne on 14 July 1921 (see pages 54, 55, 105 and 106). He is seen here in Station Street passing houses where the modern Co-op premises now stand. Throughout the visit he was enthusiastically saluted and cheered by onlookers.

THE VIEW IN CANTERBURY ROAD in the 1920s, shows the annual procession of the Sittingbourne Co-operative Society coming down from Snipeshill. The two leading horse vans displayed a variety of retail goods including mats, galvanized baths and baskets. Note the sidelights on the leading van, candle-lit with a spring in the candle tube pushing it up as the wick burnt when in use. A bread handcart is in the procession, having just passed an early motor cycle with a passenger in the low-slung side-car parked on the kerb. Across the road the shop bore the name C. Poggensee (nurseryman and florist) while on the right the garage premises displayed an 'AA' sign and advised motorists to 'Fill up here with Shell'.

A CIVIL DEFENCE FIRST AID PARTY in 1940. The members were wearing Civil Defence and St John's Ambulance Brigade badges and they used to meet at Johnson House in Burley Road on the site of the present Johnson House flats. The known identities of the group are as follows: left to right, back row, -?-, Henry Wraight, ? Rolf, 'Ern' Pratt. Front row, Bill Wheeler, ? Parker, George Harman.

ALSO IN THE DARK DAYS of 1940/41 a group of air raid wardens were stationed at the yard office of Bishop's the builders in Albany Road. This photograph was taken near the site of the new police station in the Avenue of Remembrance. Left to right, back row : -?- ; Pete Smith (of the jam factory); Percy Clinch; Vic Bourne (later landlord of the Red Lion Milstead); Jack Brisley; Hedley Butcher (builder, Ufton Lane); Alfred Rostron; -?-; Jack (?) Clinch; -?-; Alec Trollope; Harry Gouge. Middle row : Bill Hunt (Co-op undertaker); Bill (?) Gambell; -?-; Frank Bishop (builder); George Eastman; -?-; Herbert Moore (Newlands, shirt manufacturers); ? Whitnell (William Street). Front row : Albert Day; 'Jock' Ballentyne (Bowaters); -?-; -?-; Fred Moore (Bugge's Insecticides); ? Horden.

FOOTBALL MANIA took a different course in the 1930s to that of today. A regular Saturday occurance was the queue which formed in Station Street at the newsagents. The football results were phoned through to the office where they were printed in the space provided on a page of *The Evening News*. Bicycles were still a popular form of transport, the nearest of the two cars was a Standard 8 or 9 hp. The house where the 'Oxo' advert was displayed has now been replaced by a modern structure.

SECTION SIX

Shops and Pubs

AT THE END OF THE LAST CENTURY the corner site of the High Street and Crown Quay Lane was occupied by this saddler's shop, displaying a range of goods hung on the outside of the premises, where the cinema building now stands. Street corner illumination was provided by the gas-lamp standard which had a splayed foot to ward off the cartwheels of wagons cutting the corner.

THIS ILLUSTRATION reproduced from an engraving provides an earlier view than anything available in photographs. Of great interest is this view of Ballard's Hotel and Posting House which is part of the Rose Inn but separated from it by the inn yard. The copper-engraved view shows the hotel in the mid-nineteenth century when it was still one of the two main establishments in the town and an important staging post for coaches in the pre-railway era. Queen Victoria is said to have paused at the 'Rose' for lunch on her way to London to be crowned. The hotel building still exists and if you cannot immediately place it, try looking at the upper façade of Woolworths. The Rose Inn survived as an inn for many years after the demise of the hotel but eventually closed.

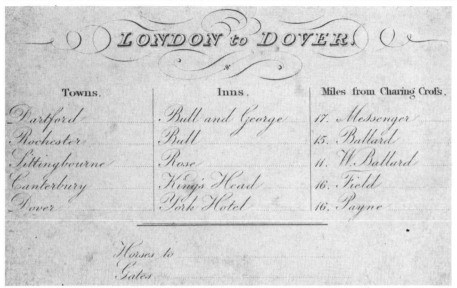

LONDON to DOVER.

Towns.	Inns.	Miles from Charing Cross.
Dartford	Bull and George	17. Messenger
Rochester	Bull	15. Ballard
Sittingbourne	Rose	11. W. Ballard
Canterbury	King's Head	16. Field
Dover	York Hotel	16. Payne

Horses to

Gates

THE REVERSE OF THE CARD shown on the opposite page provided information designed to be of use to the coach traveller of that time. There are four intermediate staging posts shown on the London to Dover route, with the distance between the points. The names of innkeepers are also shown and space at the foot of the card is given for 'Horses to' and 'Gates', the later presumably referring to toll-gates.

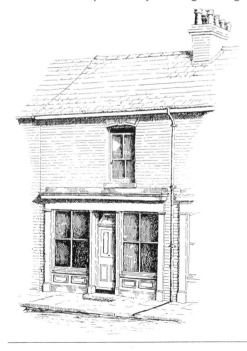

THE SITTINGBOURNE CO-OPERATIVE SOCIETY opened in 1874 with this shop in East Street. The original membership numbered 112 and £1,239 worth of goods were sold in the first year. However, the first year was troublesome to some degree. The first yearly report, from 16 February to 3 December noted 'We have a great many disagreeables ...' and called for all the support and assistance that members could give. The first manager had been dismissed, his deposit of £20 security was under consideration for forfeit to the Society. However, the business prospered and developed although as late as 1914, reference was being made to '... our triumphs over all opposition.'

THE CENTRAL PREMISES of Sittingbourne Co-operative Society in East Street are shown in this photograph of 1944, when the old premises nearest the camera were contrasted with the adjacent new building erected in 1928 bearing the motto 'Perserverance' over the main entrance. The latter year was in a period of great advancement for the Society, they also amalgamated with the Greenstreet Society, opening new premises there. In the following year of 1929 they also opened the branch in Milton Regis High Street.

A FINE WINDOW DISPLAY in 1934, probably at the Milton Regis branch of the Sittingbourne Co-op, with a kitchen cabinet used as a centrepiece. Similar items of kitchen furniture became every housewife's dream in the 1950s. They seem to fall far short of their counterpart of today – the fitted kichen – but there are still a few kitchen cabinets around and in use. The foodstuffs on display all seem enviably priced in a few (old) pennies and include oats, flour, corned beef, jam and 'Camp' coffee, with pillars of cocoa and also a pyramid of tea.

Bottom, left.
THE FIRST SHOP OF W.J. DOLDING at No. 10 West Street still forms part of the present premises which now extend further to the right. In 1912 the windows of the men's outfitters were illuminated from outside by three gas lamps on curved arms. Describing himself as a hatter and hosier on his shop sign, Mr Dolding nevertheless presented well-displayed windows with a range of men's clothing.

H. SHRUBSALL had a shop at No. 24 High Street, Sittingbourne, in around 1900. He is seen here at his doorway surrounded by a wide display of goods including bibles, reading and toy books, decorative ornaments, satchels, bags and baskets. Much space was given to an enviable array of pictorial postcards and local views. The stock he must have had would be greatly coveted today for the information depicted therein. As with many other shops of the time, outside illumination was provided by a large glass bowl enclosing a gaslight.

ANOTHER INTRIGUING SHOP FRONT in 1908 was this one at No. 21 Station Street. The London Photographic Company displayed cameras and opera glasses for sale, as well as a range of local views and specimen portraits. The firm had premises at Maidstone also and advertised themselves as 'portrait and landscape photographers'. They were also picture frame makers and dealers in photographic materials, offering the standard assurances of tradesmen of that time seeking the custom of the public, ('Highest-class work at moderate prices. Satisfaction guaranteed').

SOON AFTER THE TAKEOVER of Ridgen's Brewery in Faversham by George Beer in 1926, the name was changed to George Beer and Ridgen, and photographs were taken of the various public houses owned by the brewery. This picture of the Rose and Crown at No. 2 Bell Road, Sittingbourne, shows the newly painted and revised name of the brewery, advertising as ever, 'Kent's Best', with the old single name of Ridgen remaining in the window glass. An early motor cycle and side-car combination can be seen in the yard at the side of the premises. The building is currently in use as a restaurant.

THE FOX INN on the corner of Frognall Lane and Greenstreet at Teynham is a Victorian pub, pictured here shortly after an exterior 'facelift' in 1926. Many such establishments for years maintained a benefits club. The 'Hand-in-Hand Society' at The Fox had a membership of fifty in 1908 who met every Monday evening, providing benefits in case of sickness or death, and had a share-out in December.

ALSO IN GREENSTREET but this time on the south side of the road and therefore in Lynsted, is The George Inn situated on the corner of Lynsted Lane. The 1926 George Beer new look included, this time, a painted marble effect around the two entrances. The Maidstone & District Bus Company had a timetable on the wall, it was still a stopping place for the buses (see page 88) and the bootscrapers set in the brickwork are a reminder of earlier days when roads and paths were unpaved.

THE KING'S ARMS at No. 16 High Street, Milton Regis, was a building of late eighteenth-century appearance. This picture of 1926 shows that the step to the Private Bar was well-worn, the one in the smoking room even more so. To the right a shop offered women's blouses, one ticketed 2s.9d. (13¾p). To the left men lounged on the windowsill of a house, perhaps waiting for opening time. The site is now occupied by Ridgens Court, a private residential development. The shop building to the right survives, being London House, built c.1884.

THE BULL HOTEL is seen in Sittingbourne High Street opposite The Rose Inn and the old Ballards Hotel building in this photograph taken in the first decade of this century (see page 110). The Bull Hotel as an establishment has a recorded history dating from the fourteenth century. It remains a central establishment in the High Street and, although long past its halcyon days of servicing the stage-coaches journeying between London and Dover, it has recently been refurbished and continues to serve the thirsty passer-by. The former Bull Yard is now a pedestrian precinct. When this picture was taken its use had progressed from servicing horses to servicing the newly-appearing motor-cars.

Bottom, left.

THE WOOLPACK INN, The Street, Iwade, on the road to Kingsferry and Sheppey. This photograph was also taken in 1926 following the George Beer acquisition. The poster to the left of the building advertised the East Kent Gazette in May of that year. The paper featured an article on the aftermath of the General Strike which had just ended, and also headlined a Kent County Council rate increase of 2d. The Woolpack still offers a warm welcome to those who care to escape the thundering charge of the Sheerness ferry traffic through the narrow street.

SITUATED AT THE BOTTOM OF CHEQUERS HILL, DODDINGTON, the Chequers Inn is of great antiquity, the level of the floor inside 'the snug' and 'public' is considerably lower than that of the road outside. (A circumstance which has led to interesting and spectacular results in times of heavy rainstorms.) The thatched barn at the rear was once used for village functions before a converted chapel became available for use as a hall. The barn was destroyed by fire in the late 1960s following the careless disposal of ashes from a raked-out hearth. The pond has been filled in and the area is now used for car parking. The roof of the Chequers has been used for purposes in the past which have caused much conjecture in the present. One very probable use was for the storage of smuggled materials, for several local families of around 1800 are believed to have had an interest in avoiding excise duty on certain desirable goods.

Fire and Ambulance

FOR OVER FOUR DECADES until the Second World War, Sittingbourne Fire Brigade was guided and developed by Hedley Peters senior, followed by his son of the same name. It is H.P. sen. who appears in these pages, in addition to illustrations which also feature the Milton and Teynham brigades. This photograph shows Hedley Peters beside the new horse-drawn steam fire-engine made by Shand Mason and obtained by the town in 1898.

THE NEW SHAND MASON ENGINE was acquired by public subscription for £220 on 8 June 1898. The Chairman of the Council, christened the engine 'Victoria' by smashing a bottle of champagne on it and a demonstration of the engine's capabilities followed. Steam was raised in six minutes and a jet of water directed above the town hall. At St Michael's Church four jets were sent above the tower, then it was the 170 ft chimney shaft of the paper mill that was surpassed by the height of the water. Having soaked the highest and most prominent buildings in the town, the brigade and supporters must have been desperate for a fire, but they had a celebratory dinner in the town hall instead.

FULL MARKS FOR EFFORT to the Milton Fire Brigade in this demonstration of the effectiveness of their steam fire engine. It is uncertain whether this occasion was that of the gathering of local brigades for the arrival of the new Sittingbourne engine, but some of the atmosphere of that event is evoked in this scene of smoke, steam and spray, with three jets of water being sent high in the air before a suitably impressed crowd of onlookers. The gleaming helmets of the firemen and brasswork of the engine all enhanced a scene that must have found potential recruits in the crowd.

Bottom, left.
THE ARRIVAL of Sittingbourne's new fire engine on the occasion referred to above, is seen here leading the parade of neighbouring brigades down the High Street past St Michael's church.

WHEN HEDLEY PETERS took command of the fire brigade in Sittingbourne it was poorly equipped without even a pump. He first took in hand the town council who provided a hand cart, hose and ladder in 1897. As described earlier the pump was obtained the following year. This picture of the hose-cart team was taken at a competition in 1902.

THE ENGINE with a team of two horses was pictured in Albany Road in the same year as above, next to what is now the Recreation Ground where the team had been demonstrating their skills. A point of note is the wicker basket used as a coarse filter over the end of the hose when pumping water from sources such as ponds, and it is a device still available to brigades today. The horses were supplemented with an additional pair when the brigade was called to fires outside the town.

NEW MANAGEMENT and new equipment combined with new enthusiasm. The Sittingbourne Brigade began to win drill competitions and their first success at Tonbridge in 1901 resulted in this photograph being taken of the triumphant team with their trophies.

THE SITTINGBOURNE BRIGADE won the Steamer Drill section of the NFBU South-East District (i.e. Kent) competition in 1903 and are pictured here following that success. They completed three such wins in four years and in 1907 were champions in the three sections of steamer drill, hose cart and ambulance. Hedley Peters is seen standing on the left in front of the large wheel and on his right, i.e. the far left of the picture, was the Honorary Medical Officer.

HEDLEY PETERS SEN. remained Chief Fire Officer at Sittingbourne from 1897 to 1931. In 1930 a new motorized fire engine was bought for a cost of £1,200. It was displayed at the fire station in Crescent Street just off the High Street in the area of the present Forum Centre. The building was decorated for the occasion. The details of the crowd are not without interest for they reveal ladies' hats and coats, for instance, which are typical of the period.

HEDLEY PETERS posed his team for their likeness with the new engine, having cleared the area of spectators (except for one persistent rain-coated gremlin at the back). This 50 hp, 400 gallons per minute pump could also travel at 45 miles per hour. Times had changed since H.P. had joined the brigade in 1896, in the 300ft leather hose but no pump days. The new motor fire-engine was named 'Hedley' and Capt. Hedley Peters retired from his position as Chief Officer in 1931, handing over to his son, Hedley Peters jun. The brigades of Sittingbourne and Milton had been combined following the amalgamation of the two Urban Districts in the previous year.

THE OLD SHAND MASON STEAMER remained in service at Sittingbourne for over 30 years. In the First World War horses had become scarce and the steamer was towed by a motor vehicle bought and converted to use as a towing tractor. In 1923 a new 'Vulcan' tractor was bought as a tender and tow vehicle for the steam pump, which was performing better than ever in company with its crew who were winning competitions against brigades from all over Great Britain. The 'Vulcan' name plate can be seen in this picture on the side of the bonnet of the tractor which was also used as a tender. Captain Hedley Peters was pictured here with his son and eventual successor, and the members of the Sittingbourne Brigade with some of their trophies.

MR AND MRS G.H. DEAN of 'Whitehall' (see pages 105, 106) presented a new motor ambulance to the town on the 24 March 1913. It was not only the first in Sittingbourne, it was the first in Kent. The ambulance was built at Tunbridge Wells, with a 12/16 hp engine, solid rubber wheels, and capable of travelling at 30 mph, at which speed any patients being transported would probably have bounced a little. However, it was doubtless a great improvement over the horse-drawn ambulances previously available. These, and the new motor ambulance were all under the control of the fire brigade, whose members received regular training in first aid and wore a red cross badge. The arrival of the new ambulance was treated in the now established brigade welcoming fashion. They gave a demonstration to the assembled crowd, provided treatment to a 'wounded' man, fired a maroon and removed the patient to 'hospital'. Mr and Mrs Dean were in the forefront of the group outside the old town hall and the brigade CO, Hedley Peters, may be seen standing near the rear of the vehicle.

DURING THE FIRST WORLD WAR Captain Hedley Peters pleaded the cause of widows and orphans of firemen who had lost their lives while driving ambulances in France or on duty at home. On 18 August 1917 the Sitttingbourne and Milton Brigades combined with the Teynham and Lynsted Brigade in promoting a flag day to raise money for the cause. Parades and demonstrations around the town were only briefly interrupted by the hurried departure of the Sittingbourne tractor-drawn steam fire-engine to extinguish a real stack fire at Keycol Hill. On their return they demonstrated their engine by again directing powerful jets of water against the long-suffering tower of St Michael's Church and afterwards the tractor pulled the steamer around the town sounding its gong. Great efforts were also made in Milton Regis where a number of fundraising ventures were in hand and a fair was set up. At the latter a figure of 'Kaiser Bill' was the target in addition to the traditional coconuts. These efforts, together with those of Murston, Teynham and Lynsted resulted in a total collection on the day of £171 4s.1d. which was forwarded to the Widows' and Orphans' Fund of the NFBU. Displayed at their fire station on the day were the Sittingbourne Brigade with their steamer and tractor unit, and ambulance. Capt. Hedley Peters stood on the left before the tractor, Mrs Peters stood at the small table in front of which was a National Fire Brigades' Union poster.

HEDLEY PETERS acquired No. 93 High Street, Sittingbourne in 1902. He both lived there and conducted his business as estate agent and auctioneer from there. The premises had a large garden to the rear and Chief Officer Hedley Peters had the fire brigade pose for photographs on a number of occasions in the garden which provided an ideal background. Here the team are seen in a carefully composed group in 1911 with some of the many cups and shields they had won in competitions.

FOR THE FIRE BRIGADE, competitions and training had one object in mind, to improve efficiency at the scene of real fires and these occurred often enough as in any town. On 5 January 1907, Lloyds Paper Mill was badly damaged by a fire, pictured here from the railway embankment. The steam fire engine and tractor may be seen in the foreground next to an ample water supply.

THIS SCENE inside part of the paper mill, after the fire, shows the devastation to machinery and manufactured rolls of paper, some of which can be seen in tattered disarray. Even though the Sittingbourne Fire Brigade had made great progress in the previous few years by re-equipping and improving their efficiency, the level of equipment available to them in situations like this was quite inadequate by today's standards.

LLOYDS MILL was the scene of three big fires during the first dozen years of Hedley Peters' control of the Sittingbourne Fire Brigade. The first was in 1900, the second in 1907 and the third in 1911. The extent of damage in the latter fire is seen here. For his efforts in controlling the blaze Capt. Hedley Peters was presented with a silver cigarette case by the grateful management of Lloyds.

SMALLER FIRES, perhaps more controllable with the Shand Mason steamer pump, still did much damage while the brigade were being alerted and before they reached the scene. On 31 July 1923 at Key Street, Capt. Hedley Peters is seen walking past a building destroyed by fire which, however, had been prevented from spreading to the neighbouring cottages. The nose of the 'Vulcan' tender and tractor unit can just be seen in the bottom right-hand corner of the picture.

ANCHOR HOUSE at Lynsted presented this fire-damaged scene in the early years of this century. The 400/500 year-old building has hung on to existence with grim obstinacy through the years, although it lost its right-hand half in the last 50 years, during which it had suffered fires and bomb damage. Recently that lost half has been replaced with an addition approaching the style of the early structure.

TEYNHAM AND LYNSTED had their own fire brigade for many years, a prominent Chief Officer being Capt. A.E. Ferris who was also a keen photographer (see page 71). In 1917 he was very busy assisting in the local area flag day (see page 129) and the Teynham team strove valiantly in competitions with some success, as shown in this photograph taken June 1925 with Capt. Ferris and his winning crew grouped with their cup in front of the fire tender.

CAPTAIN A.E. FERRIS, Chief Officer of the Teynham and Lynsted Fire Brigade pictured in 1926 in full uniform and regalia. The medals included a First World War Service Medal and the red cross sleeve badge signified the first-aid qualification which most firemen also trained for.

THE AFTERMATH OF FIRE at the old Co-operative shop in Greenstreet (see page 68). This seems to be another picture of 'one that got away'. The large riveted steel water tank presumably crashed down into the cellar from the roof during the fire. Chief Fire Officer Ferris stands top left in a commanding pose, evidently in command although wearing a slightly fed-up expression.

THE MILTON REGIS FIRE BRIGADE was well established by the end of the nineteenth century, a well-known early Captain being the Revd R. Payne Smith. In 1901 a Merryweather 300 gallon steam fire-engine was obtained and kept at Crown Road. The team of horses for pulling the steamer were stabled at the George Inn in the High Street. A note of 1908 stated that the firemen were '. . . summoned by telephone bells and by the discharge of rockets.' However, by the late 1920s the brigade had progressed to possession of a fine new 'Dennis' engine against which the brigade in full uniform posed for this photograph. Left to right, back row: Spice, Wood, Palmer, Simmonds, Knowles. Front row: -?-, Overy, Blunt, Watson, Chapman, Rook, Reves, Turner, Cory.

ON THE FORECOURT of the modern looking fire station at Milton Regis the naming ceremony of the new engine took place. The 'Dennis' tender and pump was also equipped with an extending ladder. The vehicle was named 'Mary' after Mrs Mary Maundrell, Councillor and wife of a well-known local chemist. Mrs Maundrell is seen here officially naming the engine which was manned by some of the crew with others and spectators looking on. The dress of some of the ladies is interestingly 'period' and representative of the best fashionable attire of the day.

SECTION EIGHT

Sport, Entertainment, Schools and Leisure

THE SITTINGBOURNE FOOTBALL CLUB was formed in around 1883 and acquired the present ground in 1890, then described as being at the rear of the Bull Hotel. It is a well-known location now with entrances in the Avenue of Remembrance. The team had many successes in its early years, winning cups in county and local competitions. The large building on the right of this early photograph was a brewery, later to become a laundry, then the 'Queen's' cinema.

CYCLE RACING in Bowes Park around 1900. The park was situated in the angle formed by Bell Road and Highsted Road where Grayshott Close is now. Housing development gradually overcame the area, the Lawn Tennis Club being one of the last remnants to succumb (see page 142).

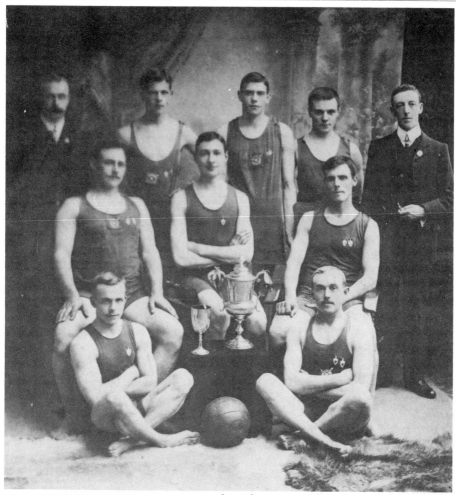

SITTINGBOURNE SWIMMING CLUB were water polo and team race champions of Kent in 1907. The successful team pictured here with their trophies were; left to right from the back, E. Smart (vice-capt.); A. Scoones; L.B. Moor; W.E. Smart; L. Smeed (Hon. Sec.); A. Bridges; G.C. Ash (Capt.); W.C. Smart; P. Seager; G.H. Clifford. The captain, George Ash, kept a bookshop and library. Percy Seager also played hockey for Gore Court, and W.E. Smart who had one forearm amputated, was nonetheless an excellent swimmer.

Bottom, left.

DR ROBERT MAXWELL BOODLE lived at 'The Chestnuts', No. 70 East Street, Sittingbourne, in a house which was one of a group built in 1790 by French refugees. Sadly most have been demolished since the last war, but this survives, still in the use of a medical practice. Dr Boodle posed for this photograph in around 1907, together with his wife and daughter, on the lawn at the rear of their house. Dr Boodle was teetotal, a revivalist and conducted temperance meetings. The excuse for including him in this 'Sport' section is that the ladies were holding croquet mallets.

SITTINGBOURNE RECREATION GROUND was first established in 1879, the ground was purchased at a cost of £2,200. In 1900 the area was increased to ten acres, following the gift of a further strip of land to the town by Mr W.J. Harris. A line of mostly young people were here suitably lined up before the summerhouse by the photographer.

THIS VIEW OF A PLEASANT PATH in the recreation ground includes a glimpse of the rustic summerhouse. The ground adjoins the cemetery and together they comprise a peaceful area, a short distance from the centre of Sittingbourne.

CUTTING THE GRASS in the recreation ground by horse-drawn mower. The war memorial shows this photograph to have been taken after 1919. At this time the cost of upkeep of the ground had probably increased, if only a little, from 1908 when the annual upkeep was £75 per annum.

THE MILTON REGIS BOWLING CLUB claims to be among the oldest in the country and the records of the club extend back as far as the reign of Queen Elizabeth I. The green is still in regular use, although it is not easy to find hidden away behind a school. The present buildings are modern, singulary unattractive affairs, but the green still looks good.

THE LAWN TENNIS CLUB between the wars had become re-established after the closure of Gore Court Archery and Lawn Tennis Club which formerly had centred on Gore Court Park. This picture of the courts and clubhouse in a surviving corner of Bowes Park was taken in the 1920/30s on the north-east side of Highsted Road near Greyshott Close. The Second World War was really responsible for the demise of the club and new houses were built on the ground.

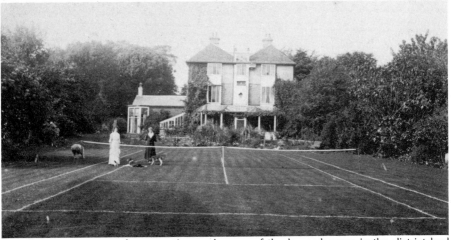

LAWN TENNIS was a popular recreation and some of the larger houses in the district had courts laid out upon their lawns. In Bredgar the well-kept lawn at the rear of Bredgar house was used in this way and the view here was taken during or a little before the First World War.

142

SITTINGBOURNE CYCLING CLUB had headquarters at the George Hotel in the High Street. Regular runs were held on Wednesday evenings and Saturday afternoons. A favoured tour was along the Canterbury Road through Bapchild, turning at Greenstreet down to Lynsted, then on to Sharsted via a much-famed avenue of beech trees returning home via Doddington. Included in this photograph were members of the Doubleday and Boulding families.

THE WILLIAM BARROW CHARITY provided funds for the building of Borden Grammar School in 1878. An attempted cost-saving exercise through brick-making on site received low marks. The bricks proved to be of low quality and were useless for the purpose. The school accommodated 130 boys, but in 1929 new premises in The Avenue of Remembrance were opened. The old building was taken over by the Kent Farm Institute, later it was used as a day training-college for teachers and now provides facilities for adult education and other purposes.

WITH ARMS OUTSTRETCHED, some sagging it must be said, as the photographer took an interminable time (or so it seemed to the boys), the pupils of the 'boys' department' stood on parade. They were in the playground of the Board Schools, Milton, erected in 1898 on the Butts and described as '. . . model scholastic buildings . . . up-to-date in every particular'. Accommodation was for 444 boys (register in 1908, 450 – average attendance 400).

UFTON LANE SCHOOL GROUP XII in around 1910. The school was built to accommodate 164 infants in 1898 for the Milton School Board. It was closed in 1972 and the building is now used for a variety of community services.

THE SCHOOL FOOTBALL TEAM of Ufton Lane School of 1929/30 prompts a smile at the boyish grins seen here, but there is also a touch of sadness. Left to right, back row: Keith Calloway; Ron Randall; Peter Mills; Sherley Cox. Front row: Ernest Stone; David Tame; Ron Simmons; (killed in action in the RAF); Jack Gregory; Ron Neaves (killed in action) Derek Dowse; Len Strouts.

THE NATIONAL CHILDREN'S HOME AND ORPHANAGE at Doddington had formerly been known at different times as; Highgate Wood Lodge, Stephenson's Convalescent Home and the Wesleyan Orphan Home. Many former children of the home remember it with affection and some even return today, nearly 50 years later, just to see the district again. It is now a County Council holiday home for handicapped children.

THE SITTINGBOURNE CHORAL SOCIETY performed many Gilbert and Sullivan operas which, as this picture shows, were elaborately costumed and provided with impressive scenery. Although many shows were given at the old Town Hall, the production of *The Yeoman of the Guard* pictured here in February 1929, was presented in the old drill hall in East Street. This building was built in 1891 and used by the 4th Battalion, The Buffs. It is now occupied by the Pentecostal Church. A few yards away is the former Methodist Church (see page 26) now used by the Sittingbourne Sports Club. The two buildings have thus suffered a strange reversal of roles.

Bottom, left.

SOME WELL-KNOWN FACES in the Sittingbourne and Faversham area in 1930 were featured in this photograph taken at the Faversham Tournament. Standing on the left was Chief Fire Officer Hedley Peters of the Sittingbourne Brigade, then Chief Officer Bradley with G. Tassell just behind. Earl Beauchamp had the trilby hat and stick, while on the far right was Lord Harris in his 79th year. Lord Harris was, of course, famed in Kent for his services to the county cricket club, both as a player and in an administrative capacity, although he had also been prominent politically in the 1890s and was a lord-in-waiting to Queen Victoria during the last five years of her reign.

THE SITTINGBOURNE INDOOR BOWLING CLUB were photographed at the opening ceremony in around 1934. The floor was laid over the swimming pool; it must have been very well done if it really was level. Among those present were S. Simpson (far left) and E.S. Boulding (second from the right).

SECTION NINE

Churches

RODMERSHAM, ST NICHOLAS CHURCH taken in around 1930 showing the fine fifteenth-century tower with much napped flintwork. The church suffered some heavy-handed restoration in the last century but preserves some treasures. The south chapel dates from around 1200 with three wooden sedilia which are a great rarity. It is a lovely place in a peaceful setting just a short distance from the modern hubbub of the town.

THE OLDEST CHURCH in Sittingbourne is St Michael's at the eastern end of the High Street. This view, taken in around 1900, probably shows more trees and shrubs in the churchyard than exist today. Unfortunately its proximity to the High Street now causes it to suffer at the hands of uncaring passers-by who often subject the place to misuse and litter. The church was badly damaged by fire in 1762 resulting in the loss of the roof (which may have been why the fire brigade used to practice heaving jets of water over the tower early this century). Eventually a full restoration was completed in the nineteenth century in which Thomas Willement had a hand with the west window of the south aisle. The niche on the external SE buttress is well-known and is thought to have formerly contained a figure of the Virgin Mary for the veneration of passing pilgrims *en route* to Canterbury. Parts of the building date from at least 1300 and there exists a list of incumbents of the parish from 1279.

Bottom, right.
THE WESLEYAN CHAPEL in Silver Street at Bredgar is pictured in this postcard taken in around 1910. This Victorian redbrick building superseded an earlier Wesleyan chapel of wood and weather-board, built in the late eighteenth century just down the road on the opposite side. It does no credit at all to Bredgar that the Victorian chapel was destroyed in 1987 and replaced by a bland private house. The earlier wooden chapel lingers on as a farm store, quietly rotting into the ground, yet it is a listed building.

THE PRESENT WESLEYAN CHURCH in the High Street replaces the former building on the same site which was destroyed by incendiary bombs in the Second World War. The earlier church, shown here in the 1900s, was distinctly Victorian in appearance, but the foundation of the Methodist movement in the district in fact extends back to the 1790s, when regular meetings were visited on at least two occasions by John Wesley, the founder of the movement.

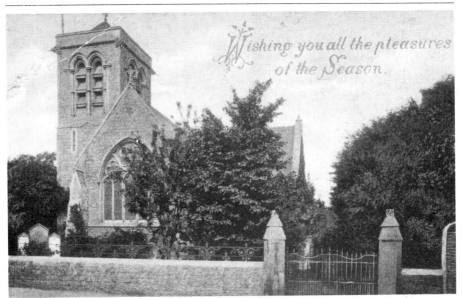

THE SECOND C. OF E. parish church in Sittingbourne is Holy Trinity in Dover Street, built in 1869 to a design of R.C. Hussey with a chancel and tower by Joseph Clarke added in 1873. The construction is mainly of Kentish ragstone and space was provided for a congregation of 640.

THE BAPTIST TABERNACLE was built at the top of Sittingbourne High Street at its continuation into West Street in 1866, with further enlargement in the 1890s 'in a wretched round-arch style.' (John Newman, *Buildings of England*) making it the biggest place of worship in Sittingbourne with room for 800 people. This scene, taken in around 1900, has added interest in the period flavour evident through the shop window display on the left, the horse traffic and the dress of passers-by.

THE BAPTIST CHURCH referred to on the previous page was the base for the very strong Baptist movement in Sittingbourne around the turn of the century. The group of church leaders, shown here in around 1908, include Mr S.S. Boulding, church deacon and secretary, who was the tallest figure standing. Also standing in the centre was Mr G.H. Dean, white bearded, check-jacketed and bow-tied, who was deacon, Sunday School superintendant, jam factory owner and local person of substance (see page 105). Seated with one arm resting on the table and wearing a long frock-coat, was the Revd John Doubleday, pastor of the church and son-in-law of Mr Dean. In 1884/5 John Doubleday married the delightful Jessie Vincent Dean who kept a fascinating diary as a young woman, living at 'Whitehall' in Bell Road. In late November 1880, the young Revd Doubleday was preaching at Sittingbourne for a trial period of a month. Jessie Dean recorded in her diary ' . . . such a beautiful sermon . . . ' in the morning of 21 November, and ' . . . another nice sermon in the evening . . . I don't know when I have enjoyed a Sunday so much'.

IN MILTON REGIS the large Congregational church was built in Crown Road in the late nineteenth century during the pastorate of the Revd William Erratt Parrett, who held the office for 26 years. The building illustrated was designed to hold 500 worshippers and replaced the original Congregational church of 1793 which was one of the earliest in the area. The church is a sorry sight now, forlorn and minus its spire, with the right-hand traceried window partly bricked up around an unsightly modern frame. At the rear a small graveyard is a disgusting mess of bonfire rubbish and rubble, amongst which are scattered fragments of gravestones. Some of the latter survive, pushed up against a wall, with dates as late as 1908 visible, '... sacred to the memory of ...'

AS AT SITTINGBOURNE the parish church at Hartlip is dedicated to St Michael. The earliest part is the chancel, dated to 1190. The ever recurring R.C. Hussey was deeply into restorations when he came here in 1864. The exterior reveals much of his guiding hand and, inside, he threw out an arch and set it in the churchyard wall. In 1902 screens and choir stalls were installed, being the gift of the Locke family. At about that date the worthy trouser-tied workman seen here was cutting the grass in the churchyard. No 'Flymo' then angrily butted gravestones and wished them out of the way.

MILTON REGIS was older in concept and bigger than Sittingbourne in its day, being favoured by Saxon kings who sometimes lived in the royal town which in itself, had developed from an earlier settlement of at least Roman times. The huge tower of Holy Trinity Church seems to be of the same date as the nave and chancel, i.e., the early fourteenth century. There is Saxon work low in the walls so the building may owe more to that period than is apparent. The extensive restoration of 1889 is generally agreed to have been well handled (significantly a local affair by W.L. Grant), although Arthur Mee mentions 48 tons of cement, ballast and reinforcing rods being necessary to tie the tower together in the 1930s. In 1908 a large pond (now filled in and with houses built on the site) was a feature of the approach to the church which was, at that time, somewhat detached from the town. The only regular service was Sunday evening during the summer months, the main life of the Church of England in Milton being centred on St Mary's in Park Road (built in 1901), now part of Sittingbourne, and St Paul's in the street of that name.

Bottom, right.
AN EARLY VIEW (c.1890) of Bobbing Church (St Bartholomew) where there is an impressive view of the Swale from the high point of the churchyard. There are Roman tiles in the fabric and their re-use, together with the prominence of the site, make the existence of an early church here very probable. Titus Oates, who later became reviled, was vicar here for a time. Of more interest to the visitor is a study of the contents of the church, including several brasses, monuments and a gorgeous piece of Romanesque sculpture.

THIS SCENE AT BORDEN CHURCH in around 1900 shows the Norman tower and doorway. The interior of the church was 'modernized' in the thirteenth century. The Dr Plot monument, c. 1696 (see page 63 bottom) is a large oval tablet surrounded by palm fronds and flowers, easily confused with that of Robert Plot, c. 1671 (the doctor's father ?). The church is in a beautiful setting and stands in a large churchyard containing many interesting headstones.

THE TENTACLES OF SITTINGBOURNE clutch at Tunstall but the church and village street just evade capture by the width of a small field. R.C. Hussey has already been mentioned in these pages and he came this way in the mid-nineteenth century. Unfortunately, he stayed long enough to 'hussle' the church into its present appearance. His saddleback top to the tower glowers above the fourteenth-century doorway below. Inside there is rather gloomy light and a disappointing monument in a side chapel.

NEWINGTON has an established early history, for it was undoubtedly favoured by Roman and Saxon inhabitants. The Church of St Mary has much of later periods, the earliest seemingly being an arcaded feature in the chancel, possibly c. 1200. It has a super tower, tall and well-proportioned with excellent knapped flintwork. The interior is long, wide and light, there are monuments, wall-paintings, brasses and much else besides. It has room for 350 persons. In 1908 things were pretty busy; two services every Sunday plus a children's service, plus Sunday School, plus HC twice a month, plus bible class (boys) at 2 p.m., bible class (girls) 2.30 p.m. (less whispering and giggles that way one supposes). For anybody with time on their hands during the week there were classes or meetings of some sort on Monday, Wednesday and Friday evenings. There was also competition from the Wesleyan Church in the village.

Bottom, left.

THE LAST STOP for spiritual refreshment this side of Sheppey, Iwade Church, has a small but early tower of thirteenth-century date. There are crown posts in the roofs and a good early planked door on the south side. Probably never regarded as important enough to be subjected to fashionable 'restoration' the building is all the better and more charming for it. Part of the rood-screen is in a chapel and there is a brass to Symon Snelling and his wife.

SUCH IS THE STOREHOUSE of history, tradition and beautiful things contained in our churches, that it is difficult to write of them in a work such as this without attempting to list the most important or attractive features likely to be of interest to a visitor with limited time. Even that is doomed to failure, for not even the smallest and most insignificant example included in the few previous pages can be given justice in a paragraph – rather a booklet of several pages would be appropriate such as is occasionally, but not often, available in the church itself. All that has been included in these pages are a few pointers to the wondrous and intriguing facets of the past encapsulated in our churches whether they be several hundred, or perhaps one hundred, years old. The illustrations included are of course merely representative of the greater number of churches in the area. Perhaps no one reading this doubts the interest value of visiting our churches. Let us do so with humility with respect for the thousands who have lived before us, and have in so many cases centred their lives on their church where they have been pleased to worship their God and maker. Inside any village church their presence is felt, those who cannot experience that then truly need the help of God. Our churches today, of whatever persuasion, face difficult times as the Church always has and doubtless always will. Nevertheless they survive in the main through the dedicated efforts of those who will never give up. Some churches become redundant, some parishes combine, to continue is hardly ever easy. Criticisms may justifiably be levelled high and low, the certain fact is that no church can survive without the support of the population. Whether we attend services or not, if we care about our churches and what they represent of the past and today, then they need our support in whatever manner we can give it and our respect when we visit them.

ACKNOWLEDGEMENTS

I have been fortunate in receiving the generous and willing help of others whose personal knowledge of Sittingbourne and district outshines my own. I am deeply indebted to those who have trustingly lent me their treasured family photographs, sometimes for a period of months, their patience and encouragement is greatly appreciated and in this vein I duly record the generosity and assistance of the following :

Mr Peter Birch • Dr Raymond Birch • Mr & Mrs P. Bushell • Mr & Mrs C. Clark • Mrs K. Dolding • Mrs Dorothy Elvy • Mrs Jessie Ferrett Mr Vic Franklin • Mr A.R. Godfrey • Mr & Mrs M. Mesher • Mr Peter Morgan Mr Edward Peters • Mr Michael Peters • Mr F.T. Reeves • Mr Antony Swain Mrs Audrey Swain • Mr N. Redman, Archivist and Mr Arthur Willis, Packaging and Warehouse Manager, Messrs Whitbread & Co. PLC.

To all others who have assisted me in any way, my thanks are also sincerely recorded.